Implications of Modern Decision Science for Military Decision-Support Systems

Paul K. Davis

Jonathan Kulick

Michael Egner

Prepared for the United States Air Force

PROJECT AIR FORCE

The research reported here was sponsored by the United States Air Force under Contract F49642-01-0-0003. Further information may be obtained from the Strategic Planning Division, Directorate of Plans, Hq USAF.

Library of Congress Cataloging-in-Publication Data

Davis, Paul K., 1943–
    Implications of modern decision science for military decision-support systems /
Paul K. Davis, Jonathan Kulick, Michael Egner.
      p. cm.
    Includes bibliographical references.
    "MG-360."
    ISBN 0-8330-3808-7 (pbk. : alk. paper)
      1. Military planning—United States—Decision making—Data processing. 2.
Decision support systems. 3. United States. Air Force—Research. I. Kulick,
Jonathan, 1966– II. Egner, Michael. III. Title.

U393.5.D37 2005
358.4'07'0973—dc22

                                                                    2005013419

The RAND Corporation is a nonprofit research organization providing objective analysis and effective solutions that address the challenges facing the public and private sectors around the world. RAND's publications do not necessarily reflect the opinions of its research clients and sponsors.

RAND® is a registered trademark.

Published 2005 by the RAND Corporation
1776 Main Street, P.O. Box 2138, Santa Monica, CA 90407-2138
1200 South Hayes Street, Arlington, VA 22202-5050
201 North Craig Street, Suite 202, Pittsburgh, PA 15213-1516
RAND URL: http://www.rand.org/
To order RAND documents or to obtain additional information, contact
Distribution Services: Telephone: (310) 451-7002;
Fax: (310) 451-6915; Email: order@rand.org

Preface

This monograph was prepared in response to a request from the United States Air Force Research Laboratory (AFRL) for a study of modern decision science that would aid in its planning of research. The monograph is a selective review touching on a wide range of topics that we believe are of particular significance and relevance to the development of decision-support systems. Most of the monograph is broadly applicable.

Most of this research was conducted within RAND Project AIR FORCE, in its Aerospace Force Development Program, headed by Edward Harshberger. The monograph also includes some overlapping research accomplished in a project on high-level decision support sponsored by the Defense Advanced Research Projects Agency (DARPA).

Comments are welcome and should be addressed to the project leader, Paul K. Davis, in RAND's Santa Monica, CA, office at Paul_Davis@rand.org.

RAND Project AIR FORCE

RAND Project AIR FORCE (PAF), a division of the RAND Corporation, is the U.S. Air Force's federally funded research and development center for studies and analyses. PAF provides the Air Force with independent analyses of policy alternatives affecting the development, employment, combat readiness, and support of current and future aerospace forces. Research is performed in four programs: Aerospace Force Development; Manpower, Personnel, and Training; Resource Management; and Strategy and Doctrine.

Additional information about PAF is available on our web site at http://www.rand.org/paf.

Contents

Figures

Tables

Summary

Decision science contributes to (1) the understanding of human decisionmaking and (2) the development of methods and tools of analysis to assist that decisionmaking. This study addresses both components, albeit selectively, and suggests a number of principles and themes to be taken into account in work on decision-support systems. We discuss the decisionmaking component first, and then the analysis component. While the discussion applies broadly, we focus on military decisionmaking and support to it.

The Decisionmaking Component

There is much to report on descriptive, normative, and prescriptive research on decisionmaking (Chapter Two). Many of the foundations were laid decades ago in pioneering studies by individuals, groups, and firms; since the 1970s, we have gained an in-depth understanding of how humans depend upon heuristics that are often apt and valuable but that can also introduce unintended biases, sometimes severely undercutting the quality of decisionmaking. Over the past decade, this body of knowledge has been supplemented by the "naturalistic" school, which notes (and champions) how experts make decisions by exploiting many of the very same wired-in attributes that trouble those in the heuristics and biases school. A debate now exists as to the form that decision support should take, with doubts arising about the appropriateness of the "rational analysis paradigm" because of its unnatural fit with human cognition. Research in this domain arguably should be achieving a synthesis of knowledge across these schools. That is just beginning to occur, and this monograph suggests a number of practical suggestions consistent with such a synthesis (Chapter Five).

One aspect of synthesis is the recognition that, while commanders in the midst of battle will and should depend heavily upon intuition, their intuition can be much improved by peacetime education and training that has been structured to teach the right lessons, build the right pattern-matching skills, and *debias* the decisionmaking judgment. Traditional analysis can do much to structure that learning program, even if the techniques used for the learning itself are more naturalistic.

A second aspect of synthesis is more speculative, but it is clear from modern research that decision-support systems that rely exclusively on rational-analytic methods are often quite ineffective—even in what appear to be "analytic settings," such as peacetime decisionmaking in the Pentagon or major commands—because of the cognitive mismatch with the decisions supposedly being supported. It would seem possible, in some circumstances, to present sound analytic information in ways that would be effective and would reduce the propensity to biased judgments. How to do so is a research issue, but we present a number of initial suggestions in Chapter Five. These include artful use of "stories" packaged so as to present alternative perspectives and pros and cons suggested by more analytically structured work accomplished offline. The routine use of *alternative* adversary models can be seen as a special case. Other suggestions relate, for example, to presenting subtle statistical information in graphical ways that humans grasp quickly. This is not always straightforward, however, because the available statistical information may not be appropriate.

The Analysis Component

Turning from issues of human cognition and behavior to decisions themselves, the analysis component of decision science owes much to a classic period, roughly from the 1950s into the 1970s, during which the principal concepts of systems analysis and policy analysis were developed. These included (Chapter Three) early methods such as "taking a systems approach," assuring that an appropriately broad range of strategies is considered; "decision analysis," with its emphasis on maximizing expected utility; game theory, which considers the decisionmaking of adversaries; and cost-benefit analysis. These methods were accompanied by related tools, such as operations-research procedures for optimization. Policy analysis extended the scope of analysis and greatly improved its treatment of relatively soft factors, such as desires, emotions, and motivations; it also introduced methods, such as policy scorecards, for relating analytical results.

More recent developments are considered in Chapter Four. Some were anticipated philosophically early on but have become practical only with the advent of powerful desktop computing. Others represent an evolution of our knowledge about analysis and how to do it well.

Understanding the System and Related Modeling

One development has been an increased emphasis on building "realistic" models and simulations, including so-called virtual worlds. These are more than mere analytic constructs designed to capture just enough about a system to do system analysis; they are attempts to study, understand, and interact with the real world through models that have increasingly high fidelity in many respects. We are still in the early stages of these developments, but experiments with virtual worlds are becoming a major element of decision support. Good decision support, however, often needs analytic work at different levels of detail and from different perspectives. A challenge at the frontier of decision science is developing well-conceived *families of models and human games* that are much more rigorous and mutually informed than what have been regarded as families of models in the past. These matters are discussed briefly in Appendix B. Another major challenge is learning how to exploit the technology of modern recreational games, including massively parallel online activities.

Methods for "Out of the Box" Planning

A second development has been new methods to help in the creative and imaginative aspects of strategic planning. Three such methods are Uncertainty-Sensitive Planning (USP), Assumption-Based Planning (ABP), and "Day After . . ." games. Although there are numerous strategic-planning methods in the community, with distinct names but highly overlapping functions, we mention these because they are well documented, and from RAND experience, we know them to be effective. Successful application of these methods has typically depended more on art than on science in the past, but with experience and documentation, they have become increasingly well defined.

Planning Under Uncertainty

The developments noted above have been stimulated by an enhanced general appreciation for the vast extent of uncertainties afflicting the planning effort. To a considerable degree, earlier approaches to analysis underemphasized the uncertainties and conveyed inappropriate goals of prediction and optimization.

Complex Adaptive Systems. The emergence of the theory of *complex adaptive systems* (CAS) has had profound effects on how we view and model many systems, further increasing our humility about prediction amid uncertainty. It has sometimes been claimed that CAS cannot be controlled because of nonlinearities, but that is an overstatement; such systems may be well behaved in large domains and essentially unpredictable in others. A challenge, then, is understanding the landscape and finding ways to increase the size of the well-behaved domains. Viewing problems in this way greatly affects the form of good analysis. Modern methods and tools for decision support should be defined accordingly. As an example, displays to a commander should help him define strategies that are either in safe zones (e.g., overwhelming force) or in zones with risks that can be at least mitigated by attention to particular factors (e.g., achieving surprise, assuring support of local populations, and avoiding collateral damage that might trigger highly adverse reactions).

Evidential Reasoning. Related to planning under uncertainty is reasoning under uncertainty. Much cutting-edge work is also being done on evidential reasoning and related topics relevant to "connecting the dots" correctly. These are only touched upon in this monograph.

Planning for Adaptiveness. Because of the increased appreciation for uncertainty and the infeasibility of getting plans "right" in cases where events are simply not very predictable, modern decision science tends to emphasize planning for adaptiveness (Davis, 2002a). It is also providing associated methods and tools. These include the method of *exploratory analysis*, which forgoes prediction for a broad, synoptic view of possibilities and a search for flexible, adaptive, and robust strategies. This represents a paradigm shift in analysis. Various enabling concepts include *multiresolution modeling*, the use of *families of models and games*, and methods of exploring uncertainty both parametrically and probabilistically. *Agent-based modeling* is an important new contributor to such modeling, although it is still at an early stage of development and sometimes is severely lacking in rigor and transparency. *Bayesian-network methods* can be quite useful in agent-based modeling and related risk analysis. More top-down methods based on hierarchical decision tables are quite different and are useful in contexts such as providing support to very high-level decisionmakers. Another contributor to adaptive planning is *model composability*, which is much more difficult to achieve than software composability because the meaningfulness of connecting models (as distinct from whether the connected models "run") often depends on subtle and context-dependent assumptions that are evident not at the interfaces between models, but rather in their interiors (if at all). Thus, model components cannot be treated as black boxes when considering composability.

Capabilities-Based Planning. A special application of planning for adaptiveness in the Department of Defense (DoD) context is *capabilities-based planning* (CBP). In addition to the methods and concepts mentioned above, some new methods for CBP include conceiving programs in terms of *mission-capability packages* and assessing effectiveness using *mission-system analysis*. Both of these constructs reflect a systems perspective in which operational capability is judged poorly unless all critical components are in place, including command and control (C^2), training, platforms, weapons, and doctrine. Traditional models have not been designed to highlight such matters easily, but decision-support systems should do so. Capabilities-based planning also requires making choices within a budget; it is not a blank-check approach. An important new approach to assisting choice is the use of *portfolio-management* tools that can illuminate holes or imbalances in an investment program, encouraging shifts across what otherwise might be inviolable categories. Such shifts should reflect both objective and subjective considerations and can only seldom be based on rigorous calculations. Nonetheless, decisions can be significantly assisted by such displays. In addition, portfolio-management tools can assist with marginal analysis or chunky marginal analysis, in which one may ask about how to spend not the next dollar but the next billion dollars. Chunky marginal analysis is important when some of the alternatives require significant investment before any return is seen.

Command and Control and Networking. Modern decision science is also placing much greater emphasis on C^2 and the networking that facilitates it. Older systems analysis and policy analysis were often structured around units and platforms. Modern work is increasingly concerned with C^2 structures, processes, and mechanisms for adaptation, as well as ubiquitous networks that allow tasks to be accomplished with resources appropriate to a problem—to a given time, place, and context. Information science is playing a central role in all of this, as illustrated by the emphasis on concepts such as *shared information awareness*. This modern work involves *virtual collaboration* and operations of virtual organizations. It is largely in the domain of information science, but understanding the effects of virtual collaboration (in comparison with face-to-face collaboration) is very germane to today's problems.

Recommendations

Consideration of decisionmaking and analysis of decisions yields a number of recommendations for the design and practice of decision-support systems and for further research. Reflecting the synthesis of rational and intuitive theories of decisionmaking, decision tools should complement human strengths and counteract weaknesses through attention to features of the tools themselves, the user-tool interaction and the tool-use environment, and development of users' decisionmaking skills. In particular, the user should be able to interact with and personalize the tools at multiple levels.

Decision support should appeal to both the rational-analytic and the intuitive capabilities of the decisionmaker, with a balance of "cold" and story-based presentation of analysis and recommendations. The particular balance should depend on characteristics of the decision, the decision environment, and the decisionmaker. Decisionmaking is well supported by providing the decisionmaker access to a variety of advisors and interlocutors. Communication tools that allow for virtual decisionmaking groups can promote consideration of alternative views and a healthy skepticism.

Acknowledgments

The report has benefited from numerous discussions and collaborations with RAND colleagues and colleagues from the general technical community. We particularly appreciate the formal reviews of the draft manuscript by RAND colleague James Kahan and Professor Eugene Santos of the University of Connecticut.

Acronyms

ABP	Assumption-Based Planning
AFRL	Air Force Research Laboratory
AFSA	Air Force Studies and Analysis
AODA	Attack Operations Decision Aid
ATO	air tasking order
C^2	command and control
C^4ISR	command, control, communications, computers, intelligence, surveillance, and reconnaissance
CAS	complex adaptive systems
CBO	Congressional Budget Office
CBP	capabilities-based planning
CCRP	Command and Control Research Program
COA	course of action
DARPA	Defense Advanced Research Projects Agency
DoD	Department of Defense
DQI	data-quality information
DSS	decision-support system
EBO	effects-based operations
EBP	effects-based planning
HBP	heuristics and biases paradigm
IIASA	International Institute for Applied Systems Analysis

JFACC   Joint Force Air Component Commander
JFCOM   Joint Forces Command
JICM   Joint Integrated Contingency Model
JWAC   Joint Warfare Analysis Center
M&S   modeling and simulation
MAAP   master air-attack plan
MADGS   multiagent distributed goal satisfaction
MAUT   multiattribute utility theory
MORS   Military Operations Research Society
MRMPM   multiresolution, multiperspective modeling
NDM   naturalistic decisionmaking
NP   naturalistic paradigm
NRC   National Research Council
NSC   National Security Council
OR   operations research
OSD   Office of the Secretary of Defense
RCM   rational-choice model
SEAS   Structured Evidential Argumentation System
SEAS   System Effectiveness Analysis Simulation
USP   Uncertainty-Sensitive Planning

CHAPTER ONE

Introduction

Objective

This monograph presents a selective survey of modern decision science prepared to assist the United States Air Force Research Laboratory (AFRL) in planning its research programs and, more specifically, developing methods and tools for decision support. Our emphasis is on relatively high-level decisionmaking rather than, say, that of pilots or intelligence analysts in the midst of real-time operations. We focus largely on what the military refers to as the strategic and operational levels. This said, we also draw upon considerable tactical-level research that has lessons for our work.

Definition and Scope

Definitions are necessary in a study such as this. We take the view that science is inquiry leading to an organized body of knowledge in a subject domain. The body of knowledge includes principles and frameworks. The knowledge is meaningful and transferable, and claims made about phenomena in the subject domain are, at least in principle, testable and reproducible. With that prelude,

Decision science contributes both to the understanding of human decisionmaking and to developing methods and tools to assist that decisionmaking. The latter branch relates closely to

understanding what constitutes good decision support[1] *and how to go about providing it.*[2]

Figure 1.1 indicates the breakdown that we have used in our approach to the subject. In addressing human decisionmaking, we consider research on descriptive, normative, and prescriptive aspects (how humans actually make decisions, how they perhaps *should* make decisions, and how to go about doing so effectively, respectively). We primarily address individual-level decisionmaking, but we include some discussion of group processes and collaboration. We largely consider human decisionmaking, but we touch also upon decisionmaking in intelligent machines. In addressing concepts, methods, and

Figure 1.1
Taxonomy of Decision Science for This Study

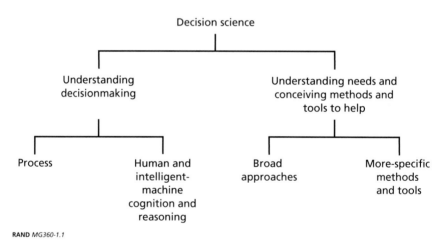

RAND *MG360-1.1*

---

[1] The term decision-support system (DSS) was apparently coined in 1971 in an article that distinguished among strategic planning, management control, and operational control and that classified decision problems as highly structured, semistructured, or unstructured (Gorry and Scott-Morton, 1971).

[2] A paper by Wayne Zachary (Zachary, 1998) identifies six generic needs: (1) projecting into the future despite uncertainty, (2) making tradeoffs among competing attributes or goals, (3) managing large amounts of information simultaneously, (4) analyzing complex situations within constraints of time and resources, (5) visualizing and manipulating those visualizations, and (6) making heuristic judgments, even if they are only qualitative.

tools, we focus primarily on relatively high-level decisionmaking, and our scope therefore tends to be associated with strategy, systems analysis, policy analysis, and choice under uncertainty.

It follows that our discussion omits a great deal that others might have included. For example, we do not address tactics, details of military targeting and maneuver, or fine-tuning resource allocation within a homogeneous domain. Nor do we deal with algorithms, computational methods, and mathematics such as might be treated in a review of operations research. Nor do we discuss many important issues of cognitive psychology, such as the performance of pilots as a function of cockpit displays. Even with these restrictions of scope, there is much to cover.

Descriptive Versus Prescriptive Research

In discussions of human decisionmaking, a distinction has often been made between descriptive and prescriptive research. The situation is actually more complex, because methods and tools intended for decision support should be cognitively comfortable for real human decisionmakers. That is not straightforward, because people do not easily reason in the manner sometimes recommended by economists or mathematicians. Furthermore, decisionmaking paradigms that once were thought to be obviously rational and good are not always as good as advertised, and they can even be dysfunctional. It turns out, then, that the frontiers of modern decision science include new concepts about what should be prescribed, not just about tools to support one style of reasoning or another.

Approach in This Monograph

A report surveying the whole of decision science would be very long and would necessarily duplicate portions of earlier books and articles. We have chosen to keep the discussion rather brief, to include what we consider useful citations to the existing literature, and to focus primarily on modern concepts and issues with which readers may be relatively unfamiliar and that have important implications for research on decision-support and related systems. Chapter Two describes some of the major findings of recent decades on how real decisionmakers actually reason and decide. This discussion reflects the "heuristics and biases" research most associated with Daniel Kahneman and Amos Tversky, and also loosely defined "naturalistic" research associated with Gary Klein, Gerd Gigerenzer, and others. The chapter also draws on research done in management schools by James March and others. Chapter Three reviews classic concepts of decision science and aspects of their evolution through the 1980s. Chapter Four discusses major themes of modern decision science. These build on the classic concepts but also repudiate the classic over-emphasis on optimization, particularly in problems characterized by deep uncertainty. The principal theme is encouraging and assisting adaptiveness. Chapter Five is a first attempt to reconcile some of the contradictory strands discussed in Chapter Two and to move toward a synthesis that might be useful to those involved in analysis and decision support; it also recapitulates our conclusions and recommendations, including recommendations for research that AFRL might reasonably pursue and suggestions for terms of reference in the development of decision-support systems.

Finally, we note that although much of the monograph is rather general, our focus is on decision science relevant to *military* decisionmaking, and many of our examples are accordingly military.

CHAPTER TWO

Human Decisionmaking

This chapter concerns the decision process and what decision science tells us about how human beings actually make decisions. Our primary emphasis is on higher-level decisionmaking, but we also draw upon literature that deals with operational decisionmaking, such as that by pilots, firemen, or platoon commanders. We do this in part because the lessons from that research extrapolate to a considerable extent to the decisionmakers on whom we have focused. We also emphasize decisionmaking by individuals. Even when decisions are made by or in groups of people and follow from interpersonal or social decision processes, the participants employ many of the same judgment and decisionmaking processes as they do when acting alone. While in no way a comprehensive treatment of judgment and decisionmaking, this chapter provides a basis for the subsequent chapters on analysis methods, as decision *support* is meaningless without supported *decisionmaking*.

How to Think About Decisionmaking

If we are to support decisionmaking, and so perhaps to improve it, we must first understand it. Despite decades of academic study, how best to think about decisionmaking remains unclear. Figure 2.1 illustrates this dilemma with four dichotomies taken from a summary work by James March (March, 1994). Should we see decisionmaking funda-

Figure 2.1
Dichotomies in Thinking About Decisionmaking

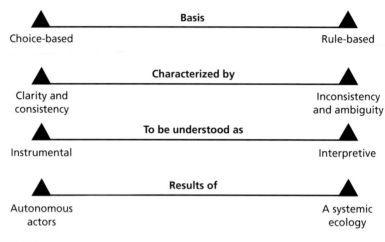

RAND *MG360-2.1*

mentally as choice-based, as in evaluating alternatives, or as rule-based, as in recognizing the pattern of a situation and responding appropriately? Should we see the decisionmaking process as one characterized by a search for clarity and consistency or as one in which inconsistency and ambiguity are not only present but exploited (as in factions agreeing on an action despite having different objectives in mind)? Should we understand decisions as fitting into problem solving and measured by an allegedly objective goodness of outcome, or do we understand them in more social terms, such as symbols of a successful negotiation, the reaffirmation of the organization's ethos, or a leader's strength? And, finally, are decisions the result of individual actors or of more complex systems?

These matters are central to our work, because if we conceive of decision support strictly in terms of "rational" action (shown on the left side of Figure 2.1), we relegate our work to that of technical support. That may provide good information but miss many of the factors that confront real decisionmakers. On the other hand, if we conceive of decision support purely in terms of facilitating natural human processes, we may be denying decisionmakers the opportunity to see sharply some of the consequences of alternatives, or to see alternatives at all. Moreover, we might reinforce cognitive biases that generate what can be seen only as errors.

Decision support has typically focused on what its practitioners see as the rational-analysis issues, with the expectation that decisionmakers themselves will fill in the other factors. Probably with good justification, practitioners of decision support have seen worrying about political factors and other soft consequences as beyond their ken, or at least beyond their pay grade. Furthermore, the ethic of much systems analysis and policy analysis has been to present clearly the more analytical perspective so that policymakers can understand fully that aspect of the problem, without "contamination" by other, more political factors, even though the other factors may be legitimate and important to the policymakers in their final decisions. In this monograph, we have taken a more expansive view of decision support, moving among extremes of the four dichotomies.

Images of the Decision Process

If we imagine decisionmaking as a relatively orderly process, we can represent it schematically as shown on the left side of Figure 2.2. Although this depiction has prominent feedback loops, the image perceived by many is nonetheless one of linearity. The right side of Figure 2.2, then, is an alternative depiction emphasizing that the actual process is anything but linear or orderly. Both versions are syntheses of classic depictions and concerns that have too often been given short shrift, notably the early steps of recognizing that a crisis is approaching and reviewing the full range of interests at stake, rather than only the most obvious.[1]

---

[1] The failure to prepare adequately for the 1990 invasion of Kuwait despite strategic warning illustrates the first problem. It can be argued that the United States and Western European states did not appreciate the importance of humanitarian considerations in the Balkans until the news media laid bare the nature of events.

Figure 2.2
An Idealized Decision Process

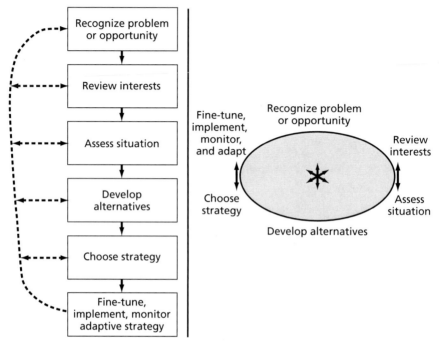

Subsequent steps—including development of alternatives, choice of strategy, and the notion of monitoring and adapting—have long been emphasized. The importance of subsequent adaptation was perhaps first acknowledged by Nobel Laureate Herbert Simon in his studies of decisionmaking in the business context and his outright rejection of then-dominant theories that imagined a more straight-forward process designed to maximize utility (expected profit). Simon recognized that high-level decisions are beset by uncertainty and that any notions of optimizing are inappropriate:

> Human behavior, even rational human behavior, is not to be accounted for by a handful of invariants. . . . Its base mecha-nisms may be relatively simple . . . but that simplicity operates in interaction with extremely complex boundary conditions imposed by the environment.

> With all of these qualifications . . . Man, faced with complexity beyond his ken, uses his information processing capacities to seek out alternatives, to resolve uncertainties, and thereby—sometimes, not always—to find ways of action that are sufficient unto the day, that satisfice (Simon, 1978, last paragraph).

A more extreme view would be that one should not even imagine optimizing, or doing a full "rational analysis," but instead should hope merely to move mostly in the right direction or even to succeed by "muddling through," as suggested by Charles Lindblom in a famous article in the late 1950s (Lindblom, 1995). The Lindblom view was that, in contrast to the normative version of decisionmaking, in which leaders assemble the options, consider all of the pros and cons, and make a reasoned judgment, reality more typically is so complex that comprehensive assessment of nonincremental options is too difficult and the result is a sequence of more hesitant steps over time. Later, Lindblom argued as well that issues are often characterized by partisan debate and compromise rather than by a more overall-rational process. Even so, the results can often be good. If Lindblom's initial work was pessimistic about doing better than just muddling through, later work by James Quinn and others suggested that indeed a firm could do better if it had an adequate vision or dream—still very far from anything like a blueprint, but strong enough to result in more than mere muddling. He referred to this process as *logical incrementalism* (Quinn, 1980).

The Problems of Heuristics and Biases

Until Simon's work in the 1950s, it was generally assumed that insofar as people engaged in orderly decisionmaking (as shown on the left sides of Figures 2.1 and 2.2), they were good at it—"good" being more or less synonymous with "rational." Simon took this standard down a notch with the notion of *bounded rationality*: In making any but the simplest decisions, we operate within a complex external environment and have limited cognitive capabilities, time, and other resources. We therefore are rational only within the bounds imposed on us (Simon, 1956, 1982a,b).

While Simon sought to bring economic man into conformity with findings in cognitive psychology, a generation of psychologists used classical economic principles such as expected-utility maximization and Bayesian probability judgments as benchmarks. They then drew inferences about cognition by observing deviations from those benchmarks (Camerer, 1995). Nobel Laureate Daniel Kahneman and the late Amos Tversky conducted the foremost experiments in this field. Their findings highlight three classes of heuristics, or cognitive shortcuts, used in making decisions (Tversky and Kahneman, 1974). The heuristics often work very well, but they can also cause trouble. The heuristics Kahneman and Tversky highlighted are discussed below.

Availability Heuristic

The perceived likelihood or frequency of an event increases with the ease of imagining it. Readily available instances or images are effectively assumed to represent unbiased estimates of statistical probabilities, even when they are not germane. For example, the USSR's Cold War assessment of the likelihood of Germany being a renascent military threat to its interests was biased by the vivid memory (availability) of World War II and the USSR's casualties in that war (Heuer, 1981). As another example, in assessing an enemy's behavior, a decisionmaker will often rely on the most available model for decision-making—his own plans and intentions. Britain based its pre–World War II estimates of the Luftwaffe's size on the basis that the "best criteria for judging Germany's rate of expansion were those that governed the rate at which the RAF could itself form efficient units" (Hinsley, Thomas, Ransom, and Knight, 1979).

Representativeness Heuristic

An object is judged to belong to a class according to how well it resembles that class (i.e., how well the object fits a stereotype of that class). This heuristic can be especially dangerous in reasoning by historical analogy (Jervis, 1976): "This situation is similar to a previous one in some important respects, so we can expect that events will proceed as they did before." For example, when policymakers in 1965 decided to deploy tens of thousands more troops in Vietnam, they had in mind historical analogies of Munich, Dien Bien Phu, and especially Korea (Khong, 1992). As Ernest May notes, "Potentially, history is an enormously rich resource for people who govern . . . [but] such people draw upon this resource haphazardly or sloppily" (May, 1973).

Anchoring and Adjustment Heuristic

A judgment is made with an initial value (anchor) in mind and is adjusted according to new information, but such adjustments are often too small, so the judgment is overweighted toward the anchor (even when the anchor is arbitrary). For example, during the Civil War Battle of Chancellorsville, Union Army General Howard once received reports early in the day, including one from his superior officer, that the enemy forces opposite his position were a covering force for a retreat (Tatarka, 2002). As the day wore on, General Howard received many reports indicating that enemy forces were in fact massing for an attack. Nevertheless, having anchored on the initial reports, he failed to adapt to the new information adequately and his corps was surprised by a Confederate attack in the evening. The Union side eventually lost the battle.

People typically use these heuristics to evaluate options, rather than attempting a complex series of estimates using Bayesian probability theory and a process of weighing costs and benefits according to multiattribute utility theory (MAUT). Again, these heuristics are often quite apt. However, they may result in a panoply of cognitive biases. Table 2.1 presents a number of examples in one cut at a taxonomy.[2] The examples are elaborated on in subsequent paragraphs,

---

[2] Note some possible confusion over nomenclature: Table 2.1 includes three biases— availability, representativeness, and anchoring—with the same names as the three classes of heuristics previously described. These biases *may* follow from the heuristics of the same name, but they do not necessarily do so.

Table 2.1
A Partial Taxonomy of Cognitive Biases

	Bias	Description
Memory	Availability	Recent or emotional events are more effectively available or retrievable by memory.
	Imaginability	Event seems probable because it is easily imagined.
	Representativeness	Event seems more probable if it is representative of its class.
	Testimony	Recalled details may be logical, coherent, and wrong.
Naïve Statistics	Base rate and chance	Normal occurrence rates may be ignored when one sees what appear to be unusual events.
	Sample size	Sample size is often ignored when inferring strength of evidence.
	Frequencies and probabilities	Equivalent data are perceived differently when they are expressed in frequencies or probabilities.
Adjustment	Anchoring	Assessments are made in relative, rather than absolute terms, even if the baseline is arbitrary.
	Conservatism	New information is accepted reluctantly or ignored.
	Regression	Events may be overweighted, ignoring likely regression to the mean.
Presentation	Framing	Events are seen differently depending on whether they are framed as gains or losses.
	False analogy	The current problem may be seen to be like a familiar one, when it is not.
	Attribution	Information may be unreasonably rejected or accepted if the source is disliked or liked, respectively.
	Order	First and last items tend to be overweighted.
	Scale	The perceived variability of data depends on scale.
Choice	Habit	An option may be chosen for its familiarity.
	Attenuation	Decisionmaking may be simplified by discounting uncertainty.
	Inconsistency	Judgments for identical cases may be inconsistent.
Confidence	Completeness	Apparently complete data may stop the search.
	Confirmation	Only confirmatory evidence may be sought, and disconfirmatory evidence may be rejected; inappropriate dissonance reduction may occur.
	Illusion of control	A sense of control may be unduly enhanced by good outcomes obtained for the wrong reasons.

and some are put into a military context in Appendix A.[3] In the aggregate, Tversky and Kahneman found that people are often poor at estimating probabilities of uncertain events (Tversky and Kahneman, 1974) and are inconsistent with respect to norms such as transitivity of preferences, even when given the correct probabilities (Tversky and Kahneman, 1981). This view of decisionmaking is sometimes called the *heuristics and biases paradigm* (HBP).

While much of the experimental work in this area involves inexperienced subjects in novel settings, the fundamental results have been borne out with experts in realistic settings (Camerer, 1995; Heuer, 1999; Hodgkinson, Brown, Maule, Glaister, and Pearman, 1999; Shafir and LeBoeuf, 2002).

Memory Biases

Selective Recall. Sometimes, we remember and use information that is either recent (the last option) or otherwise prominent in memory due to emotional content (e.g., Pearl Harbor). This bias can be the result of the availability heuristic, which is often quite valuable.

Imaginability. Participants in tense war games may later ascribe high plausibility to events of the simulated (and often highly concocted) crisis.

Testimony. People can remember events as much neater, more logical, and dramatic than they actually were. One alleged consequence is the "recovered memory syndrome," wherein people recall detailed accounts of being abused only after psychotherapy to elicit such accounts (Loftus and Ketcham, 1994).

Naïve Statistics Biases

Base Rate. Example: Clinicians place undue faith in positive test results for rare diseases, ignoring the low base rate of the disease in the

---

[3] As with heuristics, many taxonomies of cognitive biases have been adduced; the one we present here is an adaptation from Arnott (Arnott, 1998). It is useful for the content and organization of this monograph, but it is not derived from any particular theory of decision-making and is not meant to be definitive. Note that these are *un*motivated biases, as distinct from motivated biases (seeing what one wants to see), socially determined prejudices, or psychopathologies.

population and the greater likelihood that the positive result is due to a testing error.

Sample Size. People are prone to seeing patterns even when the sample size is insufficient; they may even ascribe greater significance to the result of a small sample than to that of a large sample. Sometimes the patterns seen are correct, sometimes not.

Frequencies and Probabilities. People may interpret "frequencies" more logically than they do equivalent expressions of probability.

Adjustment Biases

Anchoring and Conservatism. When assessing unusualness or goodness, people are unduly influenced by their baseline, even if the baseline is known to be arbitrary. This is consistent with *conservatism*, a reluctance to change mental models in the face of new information.

Regression to the Mean. Example: Stock-price gains in the 1990s were seen as indicative of a new era, but the bubble burst and the previous long-term average is being confirmed.

Presentation Biases

Framing. Example: An option is judged differently depending on whether it is seen as endangering an adequate baseline (betting the farm) or representing the "only way out." This is celebrated in prospect theory (Kahneman and Tversky, 1979).

False Analogy. People solve problems by drawing analogies, which are often quite wrong.

Attribution. Information may be discredited if it is attributed to someone disliked or overcredited if it is attributed to someone liked. There is a somewhat different usage of "attribution error" in social psychology, related to people attributing the cause of events or behaviors to personal character rather than circumstances.

Order and Scale. Data and options are weighted depending both on when they are presented and on the scale on which they are described.

Choice Biases

Habit. Options may be chosen simply because they are familiar and therefore deemed to be more reliable. A variant is problems being discounted because they have been seen before with no disaster occurring.

Attenuation. Decisionmaking may be unduly simplified by discounting and submerging deep uncertainty.

Confidence Biases

Completeness. Once people gain a level of confidence in an option, they not only cease looking for alternatives but are not open to them.

Confirmation. Once people have a concept of reality, and perhaps of a best option, they selectively focus on new information that confirms their view, while ignoring or rejecting contrary data. They may also seek to stamp out residual worries (i.e., to reduce dissonance). General MacArthur's unwillingness to "hear" danger signals before the Chinese invaded North Korea is a good example.

Illusion of Control. A bad choice may lead by chance to a good outcome, and a good choice may by chance lead to a bad one. When outcomes are good, they reinforce confidence and the illusion of control, which may be quite unwarranted.

The Naturalistic School

Although much of the decision literature has followed on the Kahneman-Tversky issues, that literature has come in for some serious criticism (Hogarth, 1981; Shanteau, 1989). Heuristics often yield cost-effective decisions compared with so-called rational processes that are expensive in terms of both time and mental energy. Moreover, it may not be worth even a modest effort to optimize judgment at a particular time in a dynamic problem: Changes in the situation will soon render the judgment obsolete. Some other criticisms concern the research methodology—that researchers demonstrate selection bias; that they focus on the statistical significance of biases of small magnitude; that they use contrived problems in which one interpretation is deemed normatively correct, ignoring alternative responses that may be seen as reasonable; that they elicit one-off judgments of static problem settings; and so on. More fundamentally, some critics argue that the normative standard of rationality is itself spurious, so that departures from it are not cause for concern if the judgmental biases yield outcomes that their bearers are happy with.

Some of these criticisms and a competitive view have also emerged from the empirical work of Gary Klein and Gerd Gigerenzer.[4] Klein has studied expert behavior in high-pressure decision circumstances (e.g., those of firemen and platoon commanders). This "naturalistic decisionmaking" (NDM) school[5] began, as did work on cognitive biases, by emphasizing its descriptive character. That is, it sought to describe how people actually behave, not necessarily how they should behave. Members of the school, however, have grown increasingly vociferous in presenting what they describe as a full challenger to both the rational-analytic paradigm and the emphasis on mitigating cognitive biases. Proponents argue that so-called cognitive errors reflect valuable heuristics that help humans cope with massive uncertainty and their own foibles by taking advantage of environmental clues.[6] The NDM school also argues that many of the heuristics tend to serve special human strengths, including proactive problem solving and adaptation. In contrast, they argue, the rational-analytic methods try to impose a discipline that does not fit well with

----

[4] The degree to which the two camps differ is a matter of ongoing dispute. Kahneman's review on the occasion of his Nobel Prize relates many of the criticisms of his and Tversky's work (Kahneman, 2002). A heated colloquy between the principals makes for interesting reading (Gigerenzer, 1996; Kahneman and Tversky, 1996). Chapter Five of this monograph attempts to provide a synthesis in the service of improving decision support.

[5] As a counterpoint to HBP, we will later refer to the tenets of the NDM school as the naturalistic paradigm (NP).

[6] These proponents also contend that the commonly recognized heuristics are ill-defined and specify no underlying mechanism or theory. Gigerenzer likens some of them to Rorschach inkblots (Gigerenzer, 1998). Gigerenzer's rhetoric is exaggerated; the reality of the biases is generally well confirmed. We are much more sympathetic to other aspects of the NDM school's arguments, as discussed further in Chapter Five.

human cognition—one that undercuts natural, effective decision-making.

Two of the key ideas associated with NDM are that people assess situations by using prior experience and knowledge and that situation assessment is more important than option generation. The effect is rather one of "pattern matching": People tend to solve an associated problem in the way that they "know" or "feel" is appropriate to the circumstance. For example, since instances of large classes or common events are typically easier to recall than their rarer counterparts, the availability heuristic often has considerable practical value. Indeed, *all* heuristics can enable making reasonable judgments with a minimum of effort. The resources and effort required to do marginally, if at all, better are often excessive. In this spirit, evolutionary psychology argues that heuristics have conferred advantages to those able to make decisions rapidly (Cosmides and Tooby, 1996). A different way to view the situation is that natural selection yields only *locally* optimized behaviors—i.e., better than those of one's competitors, not the best possible (Simon, 1956).

Significantly, the speed and efficiency of heuristics should not obscure their sophisticated constituent mental processes, such as pattern matching. Some contend that the "ecological rationality" of heuristics obviates the tradeoff between speed and accuracy—that is, heuristics can be both fast and optimal (Gigerenzer, Todd, and ABC Research Group, 1999).[7]

The strong version of NDM theory does not simply dismiss biases as insignificant or tolerate them as unavoidable side effects of otherwise valuable heuristics. Rather, it celebrates biases as adaptive and situation-appropriate, as does the history of scientific progress writ large. Scientists form hypotheses—often just glorified hunches—whose proof they pursue vigorously. If the evidence is lacking or disconfirming, they typically adapt the hypothesis and tack a revised course, without dwelling on the prior mismatch between theory and

---

[7] It can be argued that historical military incompetence has often not been decisive, because of adaptations, but that depending on adaptations may no longer be adequate due to changes in the nature of war (Johnson, Wrangham, and Rosen, 2002).

data. Moreover, unless the empirical evidence is compelling, they will stick with an attractive theory, one that hangs together and provides an explanation even if some empirical data tend to disconfirm it.[8] Scientific inquiry, then, does not always follow the rational-analytic model. That should cast doubt on the strong version of classical decision theory, which damns all biases as defects in decisionmaking. The strongest versions are akin to the fundamentalist approach to statistics, in which one is supposed to allow the data to speak for themselves, without contamination from theory. The results are often not very appealing, especially because they tend to lack explanatory power beyond the scope of the data.[9]

In Chapter Five, we further compare, and seek to reconcile the conflicts between, the heuristics and biases paradigm and the naturalistic school, or at least we begin the process of doing so. Classical models of decisionmaking, and related decision-support systems, leave little room for broad general knowledge and more contextual tacit knowledge and so deprive the decisionmaker of many of the benefits of experience and learning. Naturalistic models, if zealously adhered to, can fall victim to false pattern matching and can support willful deception. A synthesis is needed.

Military and National-Security Operational Decisionmaking

Decisionmaking theory has been a subject of great interest to political scientists for decades, and some of the early works on the subject are still among the best. For the national-security context, generations of university students have read Allison and Zelikow's book on the Cuban missile crisis, the second edition of which is informed by

---

[8] The role of beauty in twentieth-century theoretical physics was very strong. Nobelist Steven Weinberg writes about this candidly (Weinberg, 1994).

[9] Our point here is closely connected to the theory that says that modeling used in analysis must generate explanations of events (even "stories") if it is to be useful (Bigelow and Davis, 2003). This is also a key to model validation.

sobering post–Cold War discussions among American and Soviet leaders involved in the crisis (Allison and Zelikow, 1999). The book is a good antidote to doubts about the role of misperceptions and their potential consequences. One reads, in particular, about how—belying American beliefs during and long after the crisis—Soviet forces in Cuba had nuclear weapons and predelegated authority to use them in the event of an American attack. President Kennedy's senior advisors were largely predisposed toward military action at the outset of the crisis and even took such an outcome for granted. In the words of Paul Nitze, who was a member of the Executive Committee (ExComm) of the NSC:

> Looking back . . . at the transcripts of the early ExComm discussions, I am struck that many of us considered military action almost inevitable almost from the outset. As I recall, much of the discussion about the use of force, especially an invasion of Cuba, hinged upon whether the Soviets had already deployed nuclear warheads to the island. We operated on the assumption that it was unlikely Moscow would take such a risk, but that these could arrive at any time. As it turned out, at a conference in 1989 on the Cuban Crisis, a Soviet participant revealed that they had already delivered some warheads, so the possibility of war had been greater than suspected (Nitze, 1998).

The stakes in decisionmaking are not usually as high as those in the Cuban missile crisis, but recent events give us many examples in which the stakes have been considerable, e.g., NATO's evolving strategy for compellance of Serbia over Kosovo; the decision to project force into Afghanistan; the decision to invade Iraq; and the political and operational-level military decisions that led to rapid victory in major combat there but also contributed to severe instability in the aftermath. If a crisis ever arises with North Korea, military decisions about strategy will have profound direct and indirect effects. *How* decisions are made matters.

There is a considerable literature on military and security decisionmaking across the spectrum from tactics to grand strategy, and there is a sizable subset concerned with errors in judgment associated with excessive risk taking, or military incompetence (Dixon, 1976). The role of heuristics and biases has been explored at the highest levels of command (Jervis, Lebow, and Stein, 1985) and, to a lesser extent, at lower levels (St. John, Callan, and Proctor, 2000), but the operational level remains largely unexamined—indeed, little has been written about any aspect of modern operational theory or practice (Warden, 1989). Judgmental biases are known to be context-sensitive, and different biases are observed in different conditions, so we exercise caution in extrapolating from a well-studied domain to a largely unknown one.

Empirical research on military decisionmaking has focused almost exclusively on tactical actors and situations, up to the division command level (Serfaty, MacMillan, Entin, and Entin, 1997). An extensive research program on naval tactical decisionmaking, spawned by the USS *Vincennes* incident, has contributed to understanding its implications for effective tactical decision support (Morrison, Kelly, Moore, and Hutchins, 2000). Many retrospective studies of military operations include detailed accounts of high-level decisions (Mandeles, Hone, and Terry, 1996) and memoirs from top decisionmakers, but no similarly rigorous observational studies of high-level operational decisionmaking. General officers' time is dear, and they are not likely to be available for laboratory experiments during actual combat operations. Likewise, decisionmaking researchers are not given full access to operations centers.

More generally, experts are difficult to study. In addition to access issues, researchers are challenged to learn enough about the experts' fields to judge their performance (Fischhoff, 2002). In principle, war games could be designed to serve decisionmaking research without compromising the games' objectives, but there has been little rigorous observation on judgmental biases in operational-level games. These biases *have* been identified and studied in lower-level war games (Serfaty, Entin, and Tenney, 1989). There have also been some interesting efforts to model operational-level commanders in simulations (Sokolowski, 2003). Significantly, judgmental biases should also be reflected in adversary modeling (Barsnick, 2002). The role of such biases, especially overconfidence, is also discussed in an excellent high-level study of commanders' information needs, which focuses on the flow of information between commanders and subordinates (Kahan, Worley, and Stasz, 2000).

CHAPTER THREE

Classic Analysis Concepts and Their Evolution

Having reviewed the science on human decisionmaking, let us now turn to the aspects of decision science relating to analysis.

Depending on the discipline that one studies, the origins of "decision analysis" or related subjects may be described quite differently. Some of the strands of what we treat as classic decision science emerged in such diverse fields as economics, political science, management science, operations research, and the operational analysis of World War II. In what follows, we briefly summarize key concepts from an interdisciplinary perspective. For each concept, we provide pointers to relevant literature.

Decision Analysis and Game Theory

Decision Analysis and Utilities

The origins of decision science are unclear and ultimately indefinable because of the multiple streams of work that went on in parallel, but seminal work on game theory (von Neumann and Morgenstern, 1953) was an important part of the early history—in part, because von Neumann and Morgenstern sharpened the idea that rational choice should maximize *expected subjective utility*. Later books are much more readable and useful today, except for readers wishing to go back to the beginnings. Luce and Raiffa published a respected book in the mid-1950s that is available today in reprint (Luce and Raiffa, 1989). Raiffa also wrote an excellent primer on decision analysis in the 1960s that remains a mainstay of many university courses (Raiffa, 1968). Indeed, even the term "decision analysis," which logically covers a wider range of paradigms and methods, has become synonymous with the relatively narrow methods found in that book and others that followed. These books all utilize the classic approach of laying out decision trees, approximating the probabilities associated with events, assigning utilities to outcomes, and making choices that maximize expected utility. In a trivial example, suppose that one has several options that will lead to several outcomes with different probabilities. If U_i denotes the utility of option i, then the expected (or mean) utility of this option is given by

$$\bar{U}_i = \sum_j P(O_{ij})w_j,$$

where $P(O_{ij})$ is the assumed probability that choosing option i will lead to outcome j, and w_j is the utility of that outcome.[1] The classic prescription is that a "rational choice" is to choose among options (i = 1, 2, ...) so as to maximize expected utility.[2] This makes eminent sense to an economist thinking about making many bets, some of which will pay off and some of which will not. It is a very dubious concept to someone facing a once-in-a-lifetime decision, however, whether the issue be one of war, finance, or marriage. Nonetheless, the phrase "rational choice" is often equated to the economist's concept of maximizing expected utility.[3]

---

[1] This depiction is usually associated with single-actor decisionmaking in the absence of a thinking adversary. When an adversary does exist, it is often useful to invoke game theory, as discussed in the next subsection, rather than assigning probabilities to outcomes as though they were exogenous. In that approach, the utilities are calculated with, e.g., optimal adversary strategies.

[2] Indeed, it can be proven—given a conventional definition of rationality—that this is the optimal strategy (von Neumann and Morgenstern, 1953).

[3] Even with many betting opportunities, betting so as to maximize expected utility can be ruinous, because there will sometimes be long strings of events in which the best bet loses (persistence of bad luck). Unless one's resources are infinite, at some point the result is bankruptcy. Maximizing expected utility has long been overrated.

Other decision criteria are often better suited to individuals' or organizations' perceptions of risk, reward, and well-being and their ability to tolerate losses. It is presumptuous to call them irrational. For instance, many people place a positive value on avoiding disappointment: The "minimax regret" method entails comparing utilities with the best possible utility (regret); identifying, for each option, the maximum possible regret; and choosing the option with the smallest such maximum regret.[4] The minimax regret can be reduced even further by purchasing insurance against undesirable outcomes.

The basic ideas of decision analysis were greatly extended in the 1970s as multiattribute utility theory (MAUT), the most celebrated text for which remains that of Keeney and Raiffa (Keeney and Raiffa, 1976). Its simpler methods are so ubiquitous that we seldom think much about them today; we just use them. For business problems, the method sometimes makes sense because, ultimately, what matters is the bottom line in dollars. Various aspects of outcome can be translated into dollar implications. For example, a reliable work force means higher productivity, which translates into dollar savings. A happy and healthy work force may also translate into higher productivity and dollar savings. Thus, what began as very different kinds of issues are mapped into a common unit of utility, dollars. As a result, one might conclude in a given analysis that it would be better to spend some overhead money on a childcare facility than to save some money by buying a new piece of equipment, if the savings due to the working parents having a lower absentee rate were large enough.

As a very different example of multiattribute utility analysis, one relevant to Air Force analysis, consider a set of aircraft of three very different types (e.g., F-15E versus A-10 versus F-117A). How much is the set of aircraft worth? It is common to treat one of them as a standard (e.g., the F-15E) and to treat the others as "equivalent to" some multiple of the standard. Thus, the set might comprise ten standard aircraft, ten aircraft worth only half as much, and three aircraft worth

---

[4] For a discussion of why the criterion of minimax regret can be regarded as *morally* superior to maximizing expected utility, see Wit (1997). Although written in the context of social issues, some of the argument could be applied to national security issues as well.

twice as much. Overall capability could be roughly characterized by a score $10(1) + 10(1/2) + 3(2) = 21$. That is, the group of 23 aircraft would be characterized as equivalent to about 21 F-15Es. Obviously, developing such equivalencies requires thought. In one context, the basis might be ground vehicles destroyed in interdiction missions. A given aircraft type's "equivalency" here would be based on the product of its sortie rate and the expected kills per sortie, divided by that for the F-15E. That might be misleading, however, if avoiding losses were sufficiently important. Although it is easy to criticize such scoring methods, they can be quite valuable in many contexts. General officers, of course, must learn to think in terms of equivalencies because they need to characterize capabilities of complex forces simply.[5]

Game Theory

Game theory addresses how "rational" competitors seek to achieve outcomes reflecting their preferences. The basic concepts include "utility," which measures the satisfaction a player derives from something. This may be strongly influenced by subjective considerations, such as personal ambitions. It is sometimes assumed that a rational player, in developing a set of moves (i.e., a strategy), seeks to maximize the expected value of subjective utility,[6] but other strategies such as minimax are common. Developing a detailed strategy requires taking into account the responses of a rational competitor(s). This can be relatively simple or difficult, depending on the degree of information each player has about the status of the game and the other players' utilities. The players may need to deliberately inject some randomness into their moves.

Game theory developed in parallel with the ideas of decision analysis. Critical early concepts included distinguishing between zero-

---

[5] Use of "equivalent divisions" to characterize a mix of ground forces is an even better military example of MAUT because the units may be drastically different with respect to armor, infantry, and artillery capabilities, or with respect to their abilities for open-area maneuver or operations in close terrain.

[6] This effectively defines "rational" in this context, albeit with a recognized degree of circularity.

sum and non-zero-sum games, the latter being games in which both sides can benefit if they adopt suitable strategies. Concepts such as the Prisoner's Dilemma, Pareto equilibria, and Nash equilibria have long been part of the vocabulary of economists and analysts. In recent decades, game theory has made advances in repeated and sequential games and in deeper understanding of issues related to cooperation or noncooperation.

Describing game theory goes far beyond the scope of this monograph and would add little to the voluminous literature that is already available. Of the many published references, a book by Dixit and Nalebuff (Dixit and Nalebuff, 1991) is often recommended for its accessibility to nonspecialist readers and its examples in the social and political domains. Shorter but respectable accounts can be found online.[7]

In preparing this monograph, we also concluded that the most valuable aspects of game theory for high-level decision support are the basic concepts and structures found in the earlier works referenced in the previous subsection. It is rare, especially in higher-level decision-making, to find problems that can be *solved* analytically by game theory without doing violence to the problem.[8] The ideas and paradigms, however, have proven powerful. To be sure, determining which concepts to apply to which problems can be treacherous; a short discussion in the context of strategic planning is given by Brandenberger and Nalebuff (Brandenberger and Nalebuff, 1995).

It is not uncommon to find problems, including important military problems, in which game-theoretic approaches can be taken within computer simulations. As an example relevant to the Air Force, it is well known that simulation outcomes of theater-level conflict depend heavily on the tactics used by the combatants, greatly

---

[7] See, e.g., The Stanford Encyclopedia of Philosophy, online at http://plato.stanford.edu/entries/game-theory.

[8] In one example that still rankles, some Cold War game theorists (and military staff in war games) worked on nuclear-crisis problems by focusing on metrics such as the post-exchange ratio of nuclear weapons. Had heads of state actually obsessed on such measures, as distinct from avoiding nuclear war altogether, the world would have been even more dangerous (Davis, 1989).

complicating the use of simulations to inform decisions about alternative programs. During the Cold War, this was addressed with game-theoretic algorithms that allowed one to see results if both Red and Blue sides used their air forces "optimally" (or, at another extreme, if one or both sides instead followed nominal doctrine). This greatly reduced the scatter of outcomes and allowed analysts to measure differences among investment programs.[9]

Systems Analysis

History and Early References

Major contributions to decision science were made under the rubric of *systems analysis* between the 1950s and 1970s, many of them at RAND in work for the Air Force. The early work was strongly influenced by economists, but subsequent systems analysis has been undertaken by a diverse collection of scientists, engineers, and operations researchers. Perhaps the earliest book on the subject is one edited by Quade (Quade, 1964); a later volume was edited by Quade and Boucher (Quade and Boucher, 1968), with a still later book (Miser and Quade, 1988) representing a mature collection of articles describing not just theory, but also craft issues. A third-edition updating of earlier Quade books (Quade and Carter, 1989) is a good single volume for one's library on systems and policy analysis.[10] Since these classics were written, some of the biggest changes in Air Force operations have resulted from the emergence of stealth aircraft, precision weapons, and networking. The first two developments are easily

---

[9] Richard Hillestad led such work at RAND, developing the SAGE algorithm used in Air Force and joint studies in the 1980s. Earlier approximations trace back to the 1960s, when Lt. General Glenn Kent headed Air Force Studies and Analysis (AFSA) and then-Captain Leon Goodson worked on the problem. Later, Brigadier General Goodson headed AFSA.

[10] Other older books include one by Francis Hoeber, which has many Air Force examples (Hoeber, 1981), and one edited by Wayne Hughes, which was developed on behalf of the Military Operations Research Society (MORS) (Hughes, 1989). It includes a chapter (Friel, 1989) that discusses Air Force modeling.

treated with systems analysis; the third is something that systems analysts are still struggling to deal with well.

Defining Characteristics

Systems analysis is essentially a broad *approach*, a way of looking at problems.[11] A stylized view of systems analysis as a process is suggested in Figure 3.1, based on the early writings (e.g., Quade and

Figure 3.1
The Systems Analysis Process

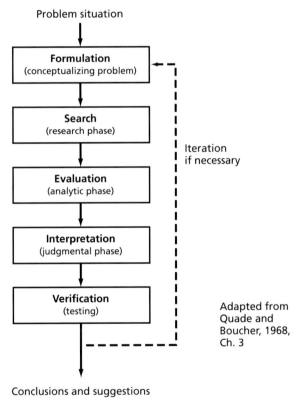

RAND *MG360-3.1*

---

[11] The term "systems analysis" has a very different meaning in software engineering, a meaning completely outside the scope of this report.

Boucher, 1968). This also relates closely to theories of idealized decisionmaking discussed in early books on the subject. An improved version of the decision process was presented in Chapter Two.

From the outset, systems analysis emphasized the importance of the following:

- Taking a "system perspective";
- Decomposing the system into parts that can be studied separately;
- Constructing a rich set of alternatives, including some that go against the grain of conventional wisdom;
- Building models to represent the system and the effects on the system of the various alternatives;
- Developing rigorous cost estimates;
- Assisting choice, based on explicit criteria.

Discussion

The domains of systems analysis and operations research overlap, and terminology is inconsistent. However, practitioners of systems analysis see it as a higher-level activity that seeks less to "solve" a mathematics problem (as in maximizing some function) than to inform decisions about what objectives to set (typically a "given" in operations research), options to be considered, and choices under uncertainty.[12]

Systems analysis calls upon game theory, decision analysis, simple modeling, simulation, and other tools. It addresses uncertainty explicitly, including uncertainty about planning factors, the enemy, and the strategic context.[13] The earliest well-known systems analysis

---

[12] James Schlesinger's definitions and distinctions, as of 1973, are quoted in Quade and Carter (1989, p. 26). Schlesinger distinguished between the economic problems of maximization, subject to control, and choice of the objectives themselves. He saw operations research as the domain of the former and systems analysis as the domain of the latter.

[13] See, e.g., the early discussions of Hitch (1966) and Quade (1966, p. 313), which note failure to deal with uncertainty *well*, despite best intentions, as one of the most deadly pitfalls of systems analysis in practice. Progress on this front is described in Chapter Four of this monograph.

study was Albert Wohlstetter's examination of basing options for the Air Force, conducted in the 1950s and described briefly in Chapter 3 of Quade's 1964 book. Systems analysis was moved into the Office of the Secretary of Defense (OSD) under Robert McNamara in 1961. Alain Enthoven headed up the new office and later wrote about how he saw its challenges and accomplishments (Enthoven and Smith, 1971). Although younger readers may be likely to have heard more criticism of this period than plaudits, the concepts and methods introduced by Enthoven had profound and laudable effects that persist to this day. One effect was that all of the military services quickly realized that they needed the capability to do convincing systems analysis.

The classic reference for the economics of systems analysis in defense planning also dates back to the 1960s (Hitch and McKean, 1965). Although early systems analysis developed measures of cost-effectiveness, it was recognized even then that simple approaches to the subject were fraught with peril. Benefits, for example, may be numerous and different in kind, not all readily reducible to dollars. Costs, moreover, can be much more difficult to characterize than one immediately recognizes. And even in simple systems, it can be difficult to ensure against double-counting costs or benefits that are correlated.

Much more sophisticated treatments of costs and benefits in systems analysis were developed in subsequent years (e.g., Fisher, 1971). Some of the ideas seem to slip away from time to time and need to be rediscovered, probably because organizations have natural tendencies to avoid some of the analysis required. For example, life-cycle costing is a fundamental concept, but one that generates a large and visible price tag that "looks worse" than merely quoting something such as the flyaway cost of an aircraft. Similarly, organizations distrust use of present-value costs, which economists often recommend.

Modern Examples

Relatively little military systems analysis is published in the public domain, for a variety of reasons, only one of which is security classification. Some papers are published in the proceedings of conferences,[14] and some can be found in *Military Operations Research Journal, Defense and Security Analysis, and Journal of Defence Science*. For published work providing case histories relevant to the Air Force, one might look at a number of studies examining aspects of the interdiction problem (e.g., Frostic, Lewis, and Bowie, 1993; Ochmanek, Harshberger, Thaler, and Kent, 1998; Davis, McEver, and Wilson, 2002). Wilkening describes an application to ballistic-missile defense (Wilkening, 1999). A recent paper (Paté-Cornell and Guikema, 2002) describes a systems analysis approach to counterterrorism, and a book by Matsumura et al. describes a decade's worth of Army-oriented analyses based on high-resolution simulation (Matsumura, Steeb, Gordon, Herbert, Glenn, and Steinberg, 2001). Finally, a recent text on "smart decisionmaking" (Hammond, Keeney, and Raiffa, 2002) summarizes many of the classic methods, particularly for business-world contexts.

Policy Analysis

History and Early References
The concepts and methods described in earlier subsections laid the basis for *policy analysis*, which has evolved steadily since the 1970s and is now a well-defined discipline with a number of degree programs at major universities.

Policy analysis uses operations research, systems analysis, cost-benefit analysis, and so on. However, it is broader than these earlier disciplines, taking into account political and organizational difficulties associated with both choices and implementation. As with systems analysis, the word "analysis" here includes not just decomposition, but the creation of problem-solving alternatives, often the result of synthesizing across boundaries (see also Quade and Carter, 1989,

---

[14] Examples include the Winter and Summer Simulation Conferences and the ORSA/TIMS conferences.

p. 5).[15] One of the early influential policy-analysis efforts was the PAWN study done by RAND for the Netherlands, a large, multiyear systems study of water-management issues; it is still an excellent case history (Goeller et al., 1983).

Defining Characteristics

Policy analysis can be defined as the systematic study of the technical and policy implications of alternative approaches to solving or mitigating public problems. It can be understood as a major extension of systems analysis (Figure 3.2), with a broader scope and a greater willingness to consider qualitative and otherwise fuzzy concerns.[16] Commonly, policy analysis includes[17]

- *Problem definition* (something often provided to an operations researcher, whose task is merely to solve the problem);
- A mix of *quantitative* and *qualitative* variables (e.g., effects on "quality of life"), perhaps evaluated subjectively;
- *Qualitative methods* such as scenario spinning, operational gaming, and Delphi techniques;[18]
- Use of *policy scorecards* in which an option is evaluated by numerous criteria that may be quite different in character ("apples and oranges," such as a policy's cost, likely effect on the number of crime incidents in a city per year, and the perceived equity of the policy among citizens);

---

[15] The work done by the International Institute for Applied Systems Analysis (IIASA) in Austria is basically the same as what we refer to as policy analysis. Many of its publications and activities are described on its website, http://www.iiasa.ac.at/.

[16] The distinctions are, of course, arguable. Some operations researchers see their field as covering systems analysis and even policy analysis. Some policy analysts do what we regard here as systems analysis or operations research.

[17] The need to include such factors was recognized fairly early by some of the pioneers of systems analysis (see Quade and Boucher, 1968). Nonetheless, these are arguably more typical of policy analysis than of systems analysis as practiced.

[18] These are summarized briefly in Chapter 11 of Quade and Carter (1989). There exists a large literature on gaming, some of it under the rubric of *strategic planning*.

Figure 3.2
Relationships Among Operations Research, Systems Analysis, and Policy Analysis

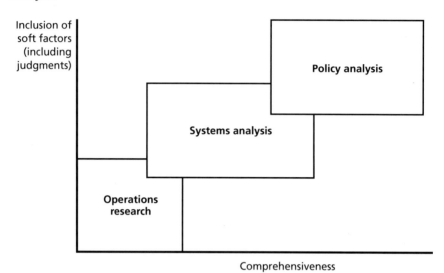

RAND *MG360-3.2*

- Aversion to simple-minded cost-effectiveness measures in preference to having decisionmakers see diverse attributes of the
  options, as is possible with *policy scorecards*. These may show, for
  example, an alternative policy's cost and likely effects in moving
  toward a variety of objectives. In social problems, these might
  include, e.g., reducing the incidence of crime and improving the
  perceived equity of the policy's law-enforcement measures
  among citizens. In defense work, objectives might correspond to
  projected success in a variety of scenarios.[19]

Discussion

As with decision analysis and systems analysis, some of the key ideas
of policy analysis are ubiquitous in today's world. *Consumer Reports*,

---

[19] Early examples of scorecards by Goeller are discussed in Quade and Carter (1989, Ch.
12). Some recent studies (Davis, Kugler, and Hillestad, 1997; Davis, 2002a; Dreyer and
Davis, forthcoming) provide examples in defense planning.

for example, makes good use of scorecard methods. To be sure, it usually has a column adding up the different considerations in some weighted manner, but the consumer sees the entire scorecard, not just some dubious rollup. Pentagon briefings make heavy use of score-cards, although quality varies enormously. In good policy analysis, such charts are rigorous in that one can understand how a given scorecard cell was evaluated (the criteria for the red/yellow/green colors are explicit) and the logic used for aggregations. For example, an option may be evaluated by a weighted sum over its attribute values (a form of decision analysis), or it may be evaluated by its weakest attribute (Hillestad and Davis, 1998). The latter approach is highly nonlinear but is also quite appropriate when viewing options for systems that are no better than their weakest critical component (Davis, 2002a). Some attributes of an option may be judged subjectively, with no pretense to rigorous quantification, but explicitly nonetheless (e.g., "Well, you and I differ in our evaluations because I am more concerned about the future peer threat than about near- and mid-term rogues"). In some instances, it is possible to aid making subjective judgments to achieve a degree of consistency in logic and scale.[20]

It might seem as though the Department of Defense (DoD) makes heavy use of both systems analysis and policy analysis, and that is to some extent true. However, there are also some sharp conflicts between best practices in policy analysis and routine DoD practice over the years. For example:

- DoD offices often insist on overquantification, even when it comes at the expense of common sense and reality. A study report may focus exclusively on measurable differences among options, even if the measuring depends on dubious models with even more dubious data, and even if "everyone knows" that there are other major considerations not being discussed. It is

---

[20] One well-known method for this is the Analytical Hierarchy Process introduced by Thomas Saaty (Saaty, 1990).

better practice in policy analysis to have all key considerations explicit, even if some of them must be evaluated subjectively.[21]

• Until the advent of effects-based operations (EBO) (Deptula, 2001), Air Force analyses were too often mechanical, focusing on tons of bombs delivered, rather than on effects achieved—not just immediate effects, but indirect and cascading effects. The work was quantitative, "rigorous," and undertaken with a systems perspective that considered logistics, combat operations, air defenses, and so on, but it sometimes fell far short of the mark when viewed against higher-level objectives.

Modern Examples

Many published studies refer to themselves as policy analysis, but most may be of little interest to readers of this monograph because they deal with social or international problems and have relatively little quantitative or otherwise overtly rigorous methodology reflecting decision science. Some examples of recent RAND policy analyses that have more of a hard-analysis flavor, while moving also well into the softer policy-analysis considerations that must be addressed by defense decisionmakers, are

• A study of ground-force options that demonstrates the short-comings of overfocusing on airliftable forces and the potential, with transformed forces, for quick operations from the sea (Gritton, Davis, Steeb, and Matsumura, 2000);

---

[21] An example recounted by Russell Murray when he was Assistant Secretary of Defense for Program Analysis and Evaluation arose some years ago when the Marines were considering the Harrier aircraft, which had notoriously poor range-payload features. Systems analysts tended to argue that the Marines should instead adopt a fixed-wing aircraft such as the F-18. That would clearly be more cost-effective in standard missions such as delivering daily tons of ordnance to targets. The Marines, however, were exceedingly worried about having assured control of their aircraft, because Marine infantry have little artillery and depend critically on timely, well-coordinated air strikes for their survival. The last thing the Marines wanted was to have their aircraft be so similar to other services' aircraft that they might be used for other missions and not be available when needed. Including that consideration on a systems-analysis viewgraph would have been unnatural to the quantitatively oriented, but in policy analysis, doing so would be quite legitimate.

- A study of rapid-deployment options for the Army, which noted the need to forward-deploy even brigade-sized units in order to achieve speed (Vick, Orletsky, Pirnie, and Jones, 2002);
- A policy analysis of command and control problems that addresses in some depth difficulties associated with organization and coordination, rather than physics (Hura, McLeod, Mesic, Sauer, Jacobs, Norton, and Hamilton, 2002);
- A study of ways to apply modern "best practices" to Air Force supply management (Moore, Baldwin, Camm, and Cook, 2002).

All of these examples use a systems approach, but they vary considerably in the techniques they bring to bear.

Another set of readily available documents illustrating policy analysis is found on the website of the Congressional Budget Office (CBO), http://www.cbo.gov. Although some CBO documents are exclusively focused on economic issues, many are substantial policy analyses. IIASA also has a great many documents available online, as well as for purchase. The IIASA documents apply almost exclusively to social-policy issues.

Summary of Classic Analysis Components of Decision Science

Table 3.1 summarizes what the classic period identified as key elements of analysis. The relationships among operations research, systems analysis, and policy analysis were suggested qualitatively above, in Figure 3.2. Policy analysis can be seen as a broadening and softening of systems analysis, which in turn builds upon but broadens operations research, including some soft factors along the way.

Table 3.1
Key Tenets of Classic Support to Decisionmaking

Tenet	Observation
Taking a "system perspective"	May include redefining the problem, tying issues together that otherwise would be treated separately, and dealing with complex interactions.
Recognizing the role of adaptive humans or human organizations in the system	May include game theory or other methods of modeling adaptive behaviors of competitors.
Decomposition of problems into workable components	May include classic methods such as objectives-to-tasks (also known as strategies-to-tasks).
Synthesis and innovation in the creation of options	Mediocre analysts may be good at decomposition, narrow cost-effectiveness, and burrowing into modules, but the best analysts are capable also of strategic thinking, imagination, synthesis, and innovation.
Assuring a suitably wide range of policy alternatives	May include innovative and initially unpopular options, as appropriate.
Quantification wherever possible: assure that variables are well-defined and measurable	The need for definition and rigor does not necessarily imply quantification, which can sometimes be a diversionary obsession.
As one component of analysis, one motivated by game theory, consider maximizing expected subjective utility	In military problems, this is often useful as a limiting case.
Minimax strategies with outcomes that are least bad across different assumptions about adversary strategy	This is often built into military doctrine as taught in staff colleges. It is not obviously appropriate in one-time problems.
Realistic, multifaceted cost estimates	Life-cycle costing, related uncertainty analysis.

CHAPTER FOUR

Advanced Decision Science for Analysis

Introduction

Structure of This Chapter

This chapter discusses some advanced features of modern decision science that contribute to systems and policy analysis. We have chosen items that appear to us to be particularly important and directly relevant to development of military decision-support systems, and on which we believe we have something useful to say. We begin by discussing several broad themes, after which we go into more detail on methods and enablers. Table 4.1 arrays the topics addressed. The organization of this chapter reflects the fact that the enablers apply to different methods and the methods apply to different themes. That is, much of what we discuss will be cross-cutting.

The broad themes we examine relate to (1) truly understanding the system under study, (2) dealing with uncertainty, and (3) working interactively and iteratively with clients.

Understanding the System

Understanding the system under study might seem an odd theme. Why is it even an issue? There are three reasons, which relate, respectively, to doing a better job in systems and policy analysis, recognizing that technology now allows us to build increasingly accurate and valuable virtual worlds, and recognizing that the way in which people learn about and discuss systems is changing.

Table 4.1
Themes, Methods, and Enablers

Themes		
Truly understanding the system	Dealing with uncertainty	Working interactively and iteratively with clients and collaborators

Methods			
Increase creativity and imagination	Enrich system modeling • System dynamics • Complex adaptive system (CAS) theory	Plan for adaptiveness	Organize around command and control and networking

Enablers				
Multiresolution modeling and families of models and games	Agent-based modeling	Modular, com-posable systems	Decision-support technology • Evidential reasoning and abduction • Risk analysis with Bayesian methods • Debiasing	Networked collaboration technologies

Improving the Quality of Higher-Level Analysis. For many years, systems analysts and policy analysts have been taught that models are highly simplified representations of some slice of reality and need be only good enough to be useful for a particular analysis. The often-quoted maxim is

> *We know that all models are bad. However, some models can at least be useful.*

Another maxim dear to the hearts of analysts is widely attributed to Albert Einstein, although we have no original source:

> *Everything should be made as simple as possible, but not simpler.*

Such maxims have long been quoted by military analysts using simple depictions of military combat, depictions such as pure attrition models in which adversary ground or air forces engage in head-to-head battle and wear each other down, often using a difference-equation version of Lanchester equations locally in the model. Analysts have argued that such a model of combat is unrealistic, but it is useful for understanding force structure issues in the large, such as whether NATO could get by during the Cold War with its then-current force structure or needed to have additional ground-force divisions and air wings. That is, even though the simulated war might have little to do with real war, it was allegedly useful for measuring the value of timely mass and firepower. One reason for the claim was that, for the military campaigns of World War II, western-front outcomes were indeed dominated by mass. It was a war fought with very large numbers of troops and sailors, between comparably capable opponents, and with relatively little art except in the early years of Blitzkrieg.

One lesson for decision science relating to analysis, arising from earlier decades of effort, is that the simple models used for many years are not adequate to support good decisionmaking today. Instead, it is often necessary to understand the target system and its phenomena in more depth than might be thought necessary by a hard-charging analyst taken by the need to keep things simple, top-down, reductionist, and suitable for economic tradeoffs. Modern developments have by no means discredited simple, high-level models, but such models need to be rooted in empirical evidence and good theory or they will omit or misrepresent important considerations that should be reflected even in an aggregate-level analysis. To be less abstract, consider how poorly pure attrition models of ground or air combat have summarized what happened in campaigns characterized by maneuver and qualitative considerations, campaigns such as the 1991 Persian Gulf war, the Israel-Syria battle over the Bekaa Valley in 1982, or the recent wars in Afghanistan and Iraq. Not only were the simple attrition models not good at description, they were also extremely misleading about resource requirements.

A key point here is that the problem is not simplicity or aggregation; the problem is developing the *right* high-level model for a given purpose. Simple high-level models may be good, or they may be insidiously appealing but quite naïve. We suggest the following rule of thumb:[1]

> *If analysis is to be accomplished largely at a given level of detail, then analysts and modelers should thoroughly understand the phenomena to at least one deeper level and recognize where even more depth is needed.*

This seemingly straightforward rule of thumb has major consequences for analysts and those providing decision support. For the examples above, they include recognizing that the relative capacities for maneuver and command and control (C^2) are *first*-order considerations that must be represented even in simple, aggregate models. The question is how to do so. That, in turn, requires understanding maneuver and C^2 in significant detail to be able to develop sound aggregate approximations of their effects. Although this need has long been recognized by good analysts, it was once very difficult to do much about it because of limitations in computers, models, and even theory.

Models remain imperfect, but aspirations can now be much higher. In best-practices work, the system in question may be modeled at several levels of detail, with the high-resolution models being accurate in important respects. For example, entity-level simulations of ground warfare represent key factors of lethality, vulnerability, terrain masking, maneuver speeds, capabilities for firing accurately at high speed, and so on. Such simulations can represent line-of-sight issues in complex urban terrain or detectability issues with semi-

---

[1] A related principle has been championed within operations research (Woolsey and Hewitt, 2003). Good operations research, even if it ultimately employs relatively simple and idealized mathematics, requires a deep understanding of the actual operations being analyzed. Thus, analysts should immerse themselves in the relevant organization and its processes before settling on a mathematical approach. That is sometimes in conflict with seeking elegant mathematics.

stealthy aircraft and advanced surface-to-air missiles. In air war, high-resolution models such as BRAWLER can treat factors such as orientation-dependence of signatures and sensor capabilities, relative maneuverability, electronic countermeasures, and even pilot capability.

So what? How does this affect higher-level models and analysis? A typical situation is one in which traditional, naïve, simple models assume that the expected value of a function is the function evaluated at the expected values of its input variables. That is, a computer model such as TACWAR or THUNDER ordinarily simulates operations using canonical values of many input variables, values that allegedly correspond to best estimates or most-likely values. If, however, one studies the underlying phenomena in more detail, one discovers that "things don't average out" (Lucas, 2000).

To the contrary, realistic estimates of outcomes may have very little to do with the canonical values of the input variables. To be less abstract, suppose that we are interested in the loss rate expected for stealthy aircraft. The losses probably have nothing to do with what happens in typical engagements; rather, they reflect the probability of certain unusual engagements in which the stealth effect is less dominant. If we have realistic high-resolution simulations with appropriately stochastic inputs, we should be able to observe such matters and construct an appropriate low-resolution model. That might have sharply different cases corresponding to whether one adversary has a dominating C^2 advantage and can therefore avoid the bad engagements (see Appendix B). That C^2 factor would not have appeared in an older, Lanchester-style conception of war.[2]

---

[2] An analogous issue exists for ground forces. If the attacker can mass his forces and prosecute a locally decisive attack before the defender can respond (a C^2 asymmetry), the effect for a large theater is roughly like doubling the minimum theater-level force ratio needed for success (e.g., from 3:1 to something like 1.25:1) (Davis, 1995). Although this phenomenon was understood qualitatively by systems analysts in the 1970s, analogous phenomena were ignored. Analyses implicitly assumed that at the tactical level, NATO's forces would be able to prevent local breakthroughs. In more-detailed simulations, one could see that results depended in uncomfortable ways on factors such as range advantages, line of sight, and the speed of advancing forces (Hillestad, Owens, and Blumenthal, 1995).

Realism is Now Feasible and Valuable. If in-depth understanding of phenomena is important for getting even high-level depictions right, it is also important for training, mission rehearsal, operations planning, and assessment of alternative weapons systems and doctrinal concepts. In earlier decades, simulations were not very realistic in many respects, and there were sharp divides between warfighters and analysts, with warfighters paying attention to map exercises and human war games, while analysts crunched numbers believed to be useful for economic decisions such as determining how much to buy.

Much has changed. Some of today's high-resolution military simulations are highly credible for certain purposes. The Army trained with them before its dramatic successes in the Persian Gulf war (Neyland, 1997), and participants said that the training was extremely useful. More generally, today's command-post exercises and experiments use a mix of high-resolution simulations and live play, with the distinctions between simulation and reality shrinking rapidly.

For the Air Force, one important aspect of modern analytical work has been demonstrated for some years by the Joint Warfare Analysis Center; this aspect is described later.

None of this means that models and simulations can reliably predict outcomes of war, because uncertainties abound, but the need to apologize for models is decreasing. Perhaps the following is not too much of an overstatement:

> *Analysts once had to understand aspects of the real world well in order to construct models that would fulfill their needs "adequately." Today, study of virtual worlds helps us understand the real world and communicate insights to be represented even in simple models.*

Military examples include mission rehearsal and distributed war gaming, which can be very similar to operational command-post preparations and, in turn, very similar to real operations with respect to C^2.[3] The simulations are becoming more and more realistic in relevant aspects, in some instances even merging with the real world (Macedonia, 2005).

Modern Computer Gaming and New Ways of Learning and Experimenting. Another dramatic change related to understanding the system well is the advent of high-quality commercial war games played worldwide, sometimes in massive online games with large numbers of simultaneous participants distributed across the Internet. Only a few years ago, these were seen by DoD as recreational activities not particularly relevant to "serious" work. Today, however, the situation is changing dramatically. One example is the America's Army game.[4] Despite looking like a commercial game and having the same type of appeal, it incorporates a great deal of realism about tactics, use of weapons, teamwork, and even the value system that the Army seeks to instill in its troops. The game has stimulated enlistments and is sometimes used by Army personnel in parallel with "real" training. For example, a soldier who has failed in real training may prepare for his next attempt by working through corresponding processes in the computer game. Although most of today's recreational war games are at the level of engagements or tactical operations, this will change as well. One issue is whether today's youth (and even older people) can learn better, faster, and with more motivation by using such games than they can in traditional ways. Currently, the intellectual base for these games is sorely lacking and would by no means constitute a military science, much less a contribution to decision science. Much potential exists, however. Both the Defense Advanced Research Projects Agency (DARPA) and the Defense Science Board have noted the significance of these developments.

---

[3] The notion that our models represent our knowledge and mechanisms of communication and are not just analytical tools is discussed in National Research Council, 1997.

[4] America's Army is the official U.S. Army game. Its website is http://www.americasarmy. com. Conceived and championed by West Point's Col. Casey Wardynski, it was originally developed by the MOVES Institute of the Naval Postgraduate School in a project led by Michael Zyda. The game is now being maintained elsewhere.

The Problem of Deep Uncertainty

The second theme for modern decision science is the need for a full appreciation of uncertainty, including deep uncertainty. A good starting point for understanding many of the methods and tools now available is the standard text by Morgan and Henrion (Morgan and Henrion, 1990). To a much greater extent than even in that text, however, decision science is coming to appreciate the *magnitude* and *depth* of uncertainty that often attend policy problems. One of the authors of this monograph has written extensively on this in the military context (Davis, 1994a, 2002a). The new paradigm here is that

> *Instead of seeking to "predict" effects on a system of various alternatives and then "optimizing" choice, it may be far better to recognize that meaningful prediction is often just not in the cards and that we should instead be seeking strategies that are flexible, adaptive, and robust.*

The move away from a focus on optimization has roots going back decades, as discussed in earlier chapters, but there are related approaches, methods, and tools of much more recent vintage.[5] We elaborate on these later in the section on the method of planning for adaptiveness.

Interaction and Iteration

A final theme relating to decision support is developing models and other analytic tools allowing *interactive* discussion with both experts looked to for information and decisionmakers being supported. Moreover, both research and the operational support of decisionmakers are increasingly making use of capabilities for *virtual discussion and collaboration*. A considerable decision science is emerging that tells us about shortcomings and strengths of such virtual meetings (Wainfan

---

[5] The earliest emphasis on "flexible, adaptive, and robust" in defense work was probably that of Davis and Finch (1993), which was improved upon in a volume on post–Cold War defense planning (Davis, 1994a,b). Both works reflected ideas developed over the previous decade (Davis and Winnefeld, 1983). RAND colleagues have emphasized the same ideas in social-policy work over the past decade (Lempert, Popper, and Bankes, 2003).

and Davis, 2004). This is of particular interest to the present authors because of a parallel project on high-level decisionmaking, one recommendation from which involves reaching out in crisis to distributed experts, advisers, and "smart people" to broaden and improve the quality of ideas available when strategies are formulated and chosen.

A Revised Process Model in the Theory of Decision Support

With these observations, Figure 4.1 suggests a revised schematic for the basic process of system analysis/policy analysis. It starts at the top by referring to *imaginative* problem definition, rather than simply accepting as sufficient the problem posed initially by the client.[6] It also adds more emphasis on understanding the system through exploratory analysis, designing a suitably broad "scenario space" (or

Figure 4.1
A Visualization of Modern Policy Analysis

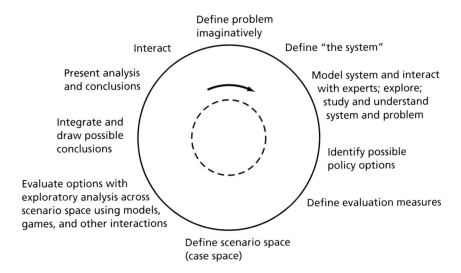

RAND *MG360-4.1*

---

[6] This has long been a theme in RAND work, as discussed in a recent book about RAND's research organizational issues by Paul Light, who came to know more about RAND's studies than most people at RAND do (Light, 2004).

case space) for that exploration, and interactions—with the client, but also with experts such as warfighters, who can suggest factors and strategies to be modeled and supplement model-based analysis with other aspects of reality. The figure shows the process moving around a circle to emphasize that it is not at all linear.[7] Especially when the goal is to predict effects rather than to optimize choice, the possible different worlds that can emerge must be considered. This orientation also takes us even further from the orthodoxy of expected-utility maximization.

Broad Methods

Against this background of themes, let us now sketch broad, related methods that are important in modern decision science for analysis.[8] As indicated in Figure 4.1, these are

- Increase creativity and imaginativeness in thinking about the problem, as in strategic planning amidst uncertainty;
- Enrich systems modeling, using ideas from systems dynamics and complex adaptive systems (CAS) theory;
- Plan for adaptiveness;
- Organize around C^2 and around networking.

Increasing Creativity and Imaginativeness in Planning

Figure 4.2 presents another variation of the idealized process of analysis and decisionmaking, one that builds in an emphasis on adaptiveness as discussed in more detail below. First, however, note how different in character some of the tasks in Figure 4.2 are. Up front in

---

[7] This figure is also consistent with recent social-policy applications of policy analysis, including those with multiple actors (van de Riet, 2003).

[8] Here and elsewhere, one could ask whether we are reviewing science or art. The answer is, "a combination." Indeed, much of "management science" can be considered art. However, our intention is to focus on points, whether art or science, that have enduring validity and are not merely current fads of business consultants.

Figure 4.2
A Revised Process Model of Analysis and Decision

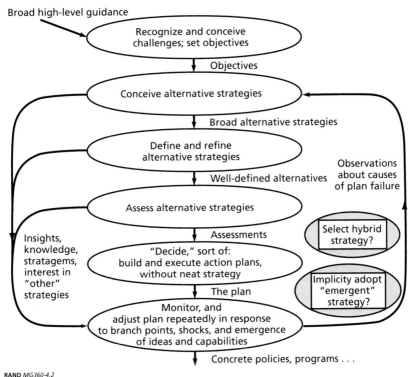

RAND *MG360-4.2*

the process (at the top of the figure), there may be a premium on
fresh, open-minded, and creative thinking about the world and about
possible objectives. In business, this phase is associated with *occasional*
big-think strategic planning of the sort that may change the nature of
a company in major ways.[9] In defense, it is associated with the
roughly once-a-decade reviews of national security strategy that may
truly be considered to be addressing "grand strategy." Usually, the
start of the process need not be so wide open, because fundamentals
are more stable. Nonetheless, it is important to recognize the need for

---

[9] We say "occasional" because organizations seldom find it useful to do this type of "out of
the box" work routinely. Indeed, routinizing strategic planning is seldom successful
(Mintzberg, 1994).

divergent, creative thinking, followed by a move to convergent high-level strategy. This need for imagination has been recognized since the classic period, when methods such as political-military war gaming, Delphi, and scenario spinning were created. However, advancements were made in the 1990s.

One report (Davis and Khalilzad, 1996) reviewed various methods from commercial practice and RAND experience and categorized them according to the *type* of planning activity to be supported.

Table 4.2 is abstracted from that study. One of the methods mentioned, Uncertainty-Sensitive Planning (USP), is particularly helpful for occasional big-think strategic planning.[10] The USP approach includes identifying branch points and potential shocks (both positive and negative) and both planning contingent responses in some detail and developing flexible capabilities to deal with the shocks for which detailed planning is impractical. Another form of "out of the box" gaming is valuable at this stage, namely, forcing participants to confront plausible bad developments outside their normal projections and then to think about how to avoid such developments. The method, used extensively at RAND, is the "Day After . . ." game introduced by Roger Molander (Millot, Molander, and Wilson, 1993; Molander, Wilson, Mussington, and Mesic, 1998).

Looking further at Figure 4.2, we see activities in which alternative strategies are framed, developed in some detail, and then tested. This is a different kind of activity; the initial part may be creative and synthetic (e.g., based on work using "concept action groups" (Birkler, Neu, and Kent, 1998)), but later the activity converges on well-defined strategies and well-defined criteria for assessment. One of the significant developments of the 1990s was recognition by James Dewar and the late Carl Builder that testing plans required something new, the ability to step outside the framework again and to ask deep questions about assumptions. A broad approach to this challenge, called Assumption-Based Planning (Dewar, 2002), has been widely applied.

---

[10] This is discussed more fully elsewhere (Davis, 2003c) and was illustrated earlier for the situation in 1992 (Davis, 1994a).

Table 4.2
Different Methods Useful in Defense Planning

Product	Methods Useful in Developing Product	Comments
National security strategy and national military strategy	Uncertainty-Sensitive Planning (USP) (Davis, 2003c)	Open-minded divergent thinking, followed by synthesis. Output can include insights affecting adaptive planning.
	Alternative futures and technology forecasts (Gordon and Nichiporuk, 1993)	Focus is on bringing out alternative images of the future with respect to both the external environment and the national strategy, and with respect to technology.
	"Day After . . ." games (Molander et al., 1998)	Purposes include thinking the unthinkable, making serious problems vivid, and conceiving new strategies.
	Assumption-Based Planning (Dewar, 2002)	Encourages creative strategy by critiquing a baseline and identifying fundamentally important but implicit assumptions that could fail.
Joint missions and operational objectives	Objectives-based planning (strategies-to-tasks) (Kent and Ochmanek, 2003)	Top-down structured analysis. Output is a taxonomy of well-defined functions to be accomplished, motivated by national strategy and its priorities and developed for a wide range of circumstances.
Joint tasks	Objectives-based planning (Kent and Simons, 1991)	Premium is on translating abstract functions into concrete tasks suitable for practical management.
Operational concepts	Concept action groups (Birkler et al., 1998)	Premium is on creative but pragmatic work producing concrete system concepts for accomplishing the various tasks and missions, followed by objective tradeoff analyses to help choose among competitive concepts.
Defense program and posture	Adaptive planning (which includes capabilities-based planning) using strategic portfolio analysis (Davis, 2002a)	Assesses programs and postures, for different budget levels, against a broad range of future contingencies (scenario-space analysis) and against needs to influence the strategic environment and be prepared for strategic adaptation.
	Strategic adaptation in complex adaptive systems (McKelvey, 1999)	Objective is to follow a hedged approach initially and to adapt in particular ways in response to specified measures of need. Purpose is to review and amend plans to better cope with uncertainty.
	Assumption-Based Planning (Dewar, 2002) Affordability analysis (Stanley, 1994)	Purposes include providing a life-cycle view of costs, timing major investments to avoid budgetary shocks or temporary losses of capability.

The lower portions of Figure 4.2 and Table 4.2 build in explicitly the concept of planning for adaptiveness, which we discuss later in this chapter, and then such practicalities of planning as objectives-to-tasks work (also called strategies-to-tasks, and associated largely with Glenn Kent) and affordability analysis (Stanley, 1994).

Enriching System Modeling

The second broad method involves enriching system modeling. At least two ways of doing so bear mention here: system dynamics and the theory of complex adaptive systems.

System Dynamics. System dynamics is a broad approach introduced by MIT's Jay Forrester in the late 1960s and early 1970s. It entails defining the system, including feedback loops that comprise decisions and adaptations, decomposing the system, developing models for the components, and reassembling—all in the context of simulations (i.e., modeling that generates predicted behaviors over time). We did not include it in Chapter Three because it did not fully catch on during the classic period and was seldom used for decision support per se. Instead, it was used in high-level studies of industrial planning, urban planning, and, eventually, global planning. Although seldom discussed by the expositors of classic systems and policy analysis, Forrester's was a brilliant pioneering effort that influenced everyone who actually bothered to read his or his students' work (Forrester, 1969; Meadows, Randers, and Meadows, 2004). It was Forrester who got through to many believers in "hard" quantification that to omit a variable from a model is typically equivalent to assuming that in the real world, the variable's effect is zero (i.e., a multiplier of one or an addition of zero). Forrester also taught effectively that the issue is not whether or not to model; it is whether to rely upon ill-posed, implicit *mental models* or to make them into real ones.

In more recent years, the system dynamics approach has been extended at MIT and coupled with convenient tools such as iThink (Sterman, 2000). One need not use the tools of system dynamics to do this type of work. For example, Analytica has been used in many such studies, including military analyses (Davis, McEver, and Wilson, 2002).

Figure 4.3 conveys many of the essential concepts of system dynamics, which fit well with the virtual-world discussion at the beginning of this chapter, although system dynamics is usually much more "analytic" and less visual in character than what we had in mind there. First, it recognizes that the real world has many unknown aspects of structure, exhibits dynamic complexity, and includes feedback effects that are often delayed. It is often very difficult or even impossible to conduct controlled experiments on the real world.

Figure 4.3
An Idealized Learning Process Consistent with System Dynamics Concepts

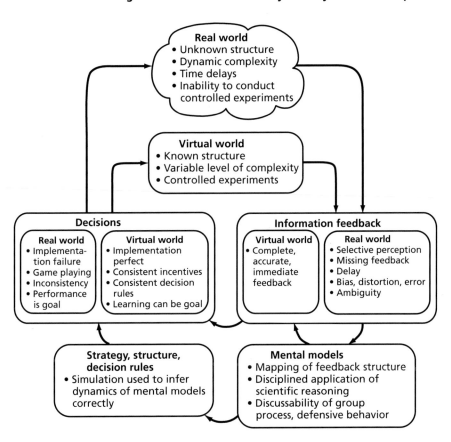

SOURCE: Adapted from Sterman (2000), Figure 1-14.
RAND MG360-4.3

Thus, we need to create virtual worlds in which we can simulate system behaviors under controlled conditions. Figure 4.3 is imperfect for our purposes, because the virtual world obviously can be extended so that it generates new structures (emergent behavior) and so that feedbacks, implementation, perception, and so on are imperfect. The point of the figure, however, is to illustrate how one can systematically seek to understand the real world through modeling and simulation.

The Theory of Complex Adaptive Systems. The second broad method is approaching systems as *complex adaptive systems* (CAS). Although its roots can be traced back at least to Poincaré, the theory largely emerged (no pun intended) in the 1980s and early 1990s. Waldrop's book (Waldrop, 1992) is a good introduction for a broad audience; it also helped publicize the work of the Santa Fe Institute, at which so much of the research has been conducted. Although many books have been written on the subject, we generally suggest reading those by the original contributors; some of these works are technically solid but not very mathematical (Holland and Mimnaugh, 1996; Holland, 1998). Other popular books give their own interesting slants on this exciting new field (Kauffman, 1993; Lewin, 2000). A short article by Brian Arthur (Arthur, 1999) describes CAS's relevance to economics. Arthur's discussion of "increasing returns to scale" (as distinct from the classic diminishing-returns concept) has been quite powerful, both in business and in military thinking about transformation. For early work, Nicolis and Prigogine (1977) is valuable but quite technical. A fairly advanced textbook by Bar-Yam (Bar-Yam, 1997) is available at http://necsi.org/publications/dcs/index.html.

Key features of CAS are typically described as some or all of the following:

- Nonlinearity and related sensitivity to initial conditions and other exogenous events in the course of time;[11]

---

[11] Interest in CAS theory has led to some misconceptions. Nonlinear systems need not be uncontrollable, much less chaotic, as evidenced by the complex linear control systems that

- "Nearly decomposable" hierarchies;
- Agents, meta-agents, and adaptation;
- Aggregation and emergent behaviors;
- Self-organization and phase transitions;
- Flow, open systems, nonequilibrium, and diversity.

Some of these terms may sound like jargon to those unfamiliar with them, but they are well explained in the sources provided above.

Although the study of CAS is not decision science, modern study of decision science would do well to adopt the concepts of CAS theory because decisionmakers are attempting to deal with complex social systems (including wars) that are, in fact, marvelous examples of CAS. Failure to do so will often encourage losing strategies, such as decision-support systems aspiring to accurate prediction. Some authors have emphasized that subjects of major interest to the military, notably effects-based operations (EBO), often need to be addressed within the CAS paradigm (Davis, 2001; Smith, 2003). A recent book provides considerable technical rigor in describing the relationship of CAS concepts to network-centric warfare (Moffat, 2003).

Note that we discuss EBO not as decision science, but as a subject that needs decision science, including CAS theory. Effects-based planning (EBP) has usually been discussed in "light" materials rather than rigorous discussions, but it is having significant effects on the way military decision problems are approached.[12] The terminology leaves much to be desired, and one may reasonably question whether there is any new concept involved (great commanders have *always*

---

exist in automobiles and dynamically unstable aircraft. As a historical point, Newton's renowned equations *are* nonlinear for most interesting systems, and while Newton himself saw the universe's activities in a mechanistic way tied to his religious notions, the nonlinearities of his laws and their consequences were studied by Poincaré.

[12] References for EBO and EBP address initial concepts (Deptula, 2001), discussion and candid review (Davis, 2001; Defense Science Board, 2003), connections to network-centric operations (Smith, 2003), Air Force applications (McCrabb, 2001), and thinking about the subject by the U.S. Joint Forces Command (JFCOM) (Dubik, 2003).

planned for effects),[13] but the effects-based approach has significantly altered the way some U.S. and NATO military organizations think, plan, and execute. Moreover, a number of core concepts and methods give it concreteness and meaning, only some of which are discussed here. Indeed, some of the most pioneering and rigorous scientific work was done by the Joint Warfare Analysis Center (JWAC), but that work is generally not in the public domain. Much of JWAC's most notable work deals with the targeting of complex physical systems, damage to which should be studied with recognition of possible substitution processes, repair, and recovery. EBO has been extended philosophically to deal with strategic issues, such as how to approach coercive bombing of an adversary leader. It can be seen as a higher-level approach, of which "rapid decisive operations" is another instance.

We shall elaborate later, so it suffices here to note that the following are highly consistent with the lessons learned from CAS theory:

- Because of nonlinearities and sensitivities, models should support exploratory analysis, rather than the search for a classic optimal solution (Davis, Bigelow, and McEver, 2001).
- Multiresolution modeling within a given model or simulation, when accompanied by the inclusion of adaptive agents (e.g., decision models representing commanders at different levels), will often be necessary to capture aspects of learning, adaptation, self-organization, and phase transitions. This may be achieved in a single self-contained model or by dynamic compositions (Davis and Bigelow, 1998).
- Dealing with qualitative and sometimes fuzzy factors is often essential and natural in representing the behavior of agents and the characteristics of uncertain, open, nonequilibrium systems (Davis, 2001; Alexander and Ross, 2002).

---

[13] Kent and Ochmanek discuss this with the Air Force in mind (Kent and Ochmanek, 2003).

Planning for Adaptiveness

Background. In practice, if not in theory, analytic decision support has often been framed as though the purpose were to choose the "correct" option. This has sometimes been seen as optimizing or satisficing across multiple, complex objectives, but in both cases it is often approached as though decisions were once and for all, and as though sufficient information were available to develop relatively detailed plans. In reality, however, decisionmakers are often faced with massive uncertainty as they make choices, those choices are revisited and modified in subsequent years, the results of plans often turn out to be significantly different from what was originally expected, and—as a last straw—the capabilities that are acquired are very often used in ways different from those originally envisioned. Strategically adaptive planning is more sensible, as emphasized in recent RAND work (Lempert, 2002; Lempert, Popper, and Bankes, 2003). De facto strategy "emerges," rather than coming about from prescient planning (Mintzberg, 1994). That notion was presaged, as noted in Chapter Two, by Lindblom and Quinn, among others.

Unfortunately, mature organizations tend to settle into comfortable routines in which strategic planning becomes a rather mechanistic activity populated by repetitive and unimaginative analyses of the same character, a continuation of past assumptions, and so on. At some point, the activity becomes a burdensome overhead; and beyond that, it may become a serious impediment to change.[14]

Within DoD, these tendencies were characterized in the 1980s and 1990s by what has come to be called threat-based planning (a misnomer for planning that relied excessively on point scenarios). The folly was in basing much planning on detailed war scenarios that were convenient for bureaucracies developing databases and running big combat models, whereas defense planning was in reality beset by

---

[14] Mintzberg discusses this especially well (Mintzberg, 1994; Mintzberg, Ahlstrand, and Lampel, 1998). Within DoD, there has long been a related concern that the Planning, Programming, and Budgeting System (PPBS) has become ossified. The new system of Planning, Programming, and Budgeting and Execution (PPBE) is an important reform effort that moves toward implementation of capabilities-based planning (CBP) (Rumsfeld, 2001).

deep uncertainties in many dimensions: who would constitute future threats, what would be the nature of combat operations, what detailed circumstances would apply at the time, and so on.

Capabilities-Based Planning as a Manifestation of Planning for Adaptiveness. Over the course of the 1990s, a good deal of thinking and research went into alternative approaches, one of which was called *planning for adaptiveness* (Davis, 1994a; Davis, Gompert, and Kugler, 1996). Some of the key ideas appeared in the Clinton administration's Quadrennial Defense Review (Cohen, 1997), but they were not backed up with tough choices. In 2001, however, Secretary of Defense Donald Rumsfeld insisted on a fundamental shift to capabilities-based planning (CBP) (Rumsfeld, 2001), which is intended to be very much a form of planning for adaptiveness (Davis, 2002a). A variety of briefings are available within DoD (Swett, 2003; Henry, 2004) describing work by the Office of the Under Secretary for Policy that is being used as the basis for Office of the Secretary of Defense (OSD) guidance documents.

Definitions. Official definitions are still evolving within the Pentagon, but one definition is

> *Capabilities-based planning is planning under uncertainty to provide capabilities suitable for a wide range of modern-day challenges and circumstances while working within an economic framework that necessitates choice* (Davis, 2002a).

In this context, "capabilities" means the general potential or wherewithal.

As so often happens in the English language, there are other meanings as well. One of the most important arises in a context such as a general asking, "Yes, that's fine, Colonel, but do you *really* have the capability to . . . if I give the go-ahead?" Here, what is at issue is whether the colonel and his forces are truly ready and able to do something, more or less "now." Having broad potential is not good enough. To avoid ambiguity, we attach the adjective "operational" when that meaning is intended. That is, the colonel might respond, "Yes sir, we have the operational capability; we're ready and able." To assess operational capability requires, in our view, close attention to "mission-system analysis" and, in investing, to what are called "mission-capability packages."[15]

Key Features of Planning for Adaptiveness. Key features of planning for adaptiveness are

- Goals of flexibility, adaptiveness, and robustness, rather than optimization;
- An emphasis on modular (building-block) capabilities that are usable in many ways and on related assembly capability;[16]
- A focus on the necessity for choice within economic constraints.

In military matters, this is in contrast with, for example, developing units, equipment, doctrine, and plans designed to do extremely well in a specific context such as a North Korean invasion of South Korea, according to standard images of how that would occur.

Exploratory Analysis. A key element of decision support in work to implement such ideas is assessing options throughout a *scenario space*, or case space, in which key assumptions are varied, sometimes substantially, in accord with the extent of true uncertainty. This is *exploratory analysis*, a method designed for broad, synoptic study of a problem area and related options. It can be considered merely to be sensitivity analysis done right, but in practice it is so different from classic sensitivity analysis as to merit a distinct designation. In classic analysis, one typically has a baseline view of the system, which is often referred to (improperly) as a best-estimate view. Then one examines consequences of changing assumptions, one or two at a time and typically on the margin (e.g., ±20 percent). This is valuable but far from sufficient, especially in problem areas beset by deep

---

[15] The mission-capability package concept has been emphasized by OSD's David Alberts for some years (Alberts, Garstka, and Stein, 1999). Mission-system analysis is discussed in Davis (2002a).

[16] For example, assuring that brigades and squadrons are configured and structured so that they can be deployed and supported independently without leaving other brigades and squadrons useless for lack of support.

uncertainty. *Many* higher-level decision problems are of this type. In defense planning, for example, there are profound uncertainties about almost everything that would determine the outcome of the next war: who the enemy would be, the political-military scenario that initiates the conflict, the size and capability of the enemy's forces (typically some years in the future), the real-world operational capabilities of one's own forces, the detailed circumstances of terrain tactics, and so on. To imagine that defense planning can be accomplished well by working through a few illustrative scenarios in detail is quite foolish, a fact that has been recognized with the advent of CBP.

In exploratory analysis, one confronts uncertainties by considering a broad range of cases and, for each, a broad range of assumptions in the various dimensions that matter—and does so by varying the assumptions *simultaneously*. In this methodology, there is no need to depend on the baseline case having any particular relationship to a best estimate. Rather, one thinks in terms of assessing capabilities over a scenario space (or case space), much as an architect or designer tests his concepts over a space of use cases and the like. Discussed in numerous papers (e.g., Davis, 1994a, 2003a), the idea is taking hold and is reflected in current OSD guidance to the services.[17]

Although tools for exploratory analysis are still not widely used, there are some good ones on the market and others in development. One of the authors of this monograph (Davis) has used Analytica extensively, after having compared it with a variety of other options used in the business world for risk analysis (e.g., At Risk and Crystal Ball, which is a plug-in supplement to Microsoft's EXCEL that allows inputs to be represented as probabilistic) and with systems such as iThink and Extend. All of these have their own advantages and disadvantages.[18]

---

[17] A related broad method is "exploratory modeling," which has been pursued at RAND by Steven Bankes (Bankes, 1993), originally more from the viewpoint of a technologist than that of an analyst, and then in social-policy analysis (Lempert, Popper, and Bankes, 2003).

[18] Documentation exists on Analytica-based military applications to Air Force problems in a joint context (McEver, Davis, and Bigelow, 2000; Davis, McEver, and Wilson, 2002). A broader discussion of its value in decision support appears in Morgan and Henrion (1990).

Portfolio-Management Methods. Another important method in planning for adaptiveness is the use of portfolio-management techniques, the purpose of which is to display for decisionmakers appropriate summary views of options for investment and to evaluate how they contribute to diverse objectives and address diverse classes of risk. Instead of using something like multiattribute utility analysis, the portfolio approach urges use of policy-analysis *scorecards*. Ideally, these are linked to model-based analysis as well as to reliable data. Decisionmakers are encouraged to think less about marginal analysis than about where there are significant gaps or "imbalances" in the overall program, as viewed against the full range of objectives. "Balance" here does not mean "equal," because hedging actions, for example, may require relatively little money and yet can be quite important. The idea is to balance risks appropriately across categories.

Portfolio methods can also be used for true marginal analysis, although most of the hard work needs to be done at staff level because details matter. Relevant tools are becoming available (e.g., Hillestad and Davis, 1998; Davis, 2002a; 2005; Dreyer and Davis, 2005).

Strategic Adaptiveness. Another aspect of planning for adaptiveness, which we refer to as planning for *strategic* adaptiveness, recognizes that challenges and contexts appear and disappear, that new technological capabilities arise, and that the course of events over a period of years is often not readily predictable or plannable. Indeed, developments sometimes "emerge" in the course of events, without prior planning.

This does not mean that planning is useless; rather, it means that an explicit concept in strategic planning should be building in the flexibility to permit adaptations (even to include the emergence of substantially new strategies, when needed). This attitude is particularly appropriate when uncertainties are profound.

Such considerations suggest a broad approach in which planners recognize explicitly that decisions now are not necessarily forever and that changes will be needed. This can be liberating, because it can permit decisions that move in what is believed to be the right direction, without overcommitting. The approach has been applied to the policy debate about global warming amidst enormous uncertainty about technological developments, the actual rate at which global warming is occurring, and the consequences of the warning (Lempert, 2002). RAND has also used this approach for the long-term planning of ballistic-missile defense.[19]

Military Operational Adaptiveness. Another form of planning for adaptiveness is exhibited by operational military commanders, who must continually adapt to unfolding events and new information. So also, C^2 decision-support systems need to accommodate their varying needs for communication and information processing as circumstances dictate. To decide and to act, the commander and his staff need to have a shared image of the battlefield and some degree of assurance that the image is correct. One RAND study (Kahan, Worley, and Stasz, 2000) found three principal modes of information processing in shared situation assessment: (1) *pipeline*—one-way transmission according to set procedures, as in a command-post decision briefing; (2) *alarm*—an unusual event or datum trips an alarm and takes precedence over ongoing communications; and (3) *tree*—the commander demands particular information from a vast base of potential interest. As the authors note:

> The need to support the three modes of information exchange imposes demands on the underlying command-and-control system. To support the commander and his staff in all three modes, the command-and-control system must be able to determine what information should be sent and when that information should be sent; it must also be able to query a large and diverse universe of information (Kahan, Worley, and Stasz, 2000, pp. 50–51).

---

[19] Practicalities often get in the way. Planners, for example, must submit budgets. If they have in mind adaptations later that might mean cancellation of some program unless it pays off, or if they have in mind having a stream of funds to be used as appropriate based on information that comes in, they may well find themselves with many problems: those who would protect the current program and those looking for "spare money" to be used for other purposes. Pots of funds for contingencies and adaptations are prime candidates for being stolen away.

Planning for adaptiveness, then, is a broad approach with profound significance.

Analogs for Intelligent Machines. Although we can only touch upon the subject in this monograph, it is significant that researchers concerned with designing and building intelligent machines, such as robots, are increasingly emphasizing many of the themes that appear here. In particular, if machines such as intelligent surveillance platforms, not to mention intelligent *armed* surveillance platforms, are to have a broad operating domain, they must be adaptive, because it is not possible to predict all of the circumstances in which they will find themselves. This arguably leads to requirements for multiresolution modeling and exploratory analysis so that courses of action will be robustly effective.[20]

Organizing Around Command and Control and Related Networking

The advent of network-centric thinking is so important a new development as to warrant being considered a broad approach in decision science. Some might argue that C^2 has always been central in military applications of decision science, but that is easily disproved by the empirical record, which demonstrates that for decades, U.S. analysis was usually organized around weapons systems, platforms, forces, and processes of war such as attrition and maneuver. Command and control was often treated—if at all—as a resource assumed adequate (e.g., good communications), as the implicit source of objectives and constraints, and as a source of friction to be represented by a few delay times. This point has long been noted, but it can also be observed directly by viewing the contents of classic books on systems analysis (e.g., Quade and Boucher, 1968). That is, the problem ran deep and affected the implicit "decision science" under which analysts operated. As a single example, consider a typical Cold War theater-level combat model. "Strategy" was represented *implicitly* in the low-level databases that scripted where various force units would go on which day and what they would do. Coordination across NATO's multi-

---

[20] See, for example, a book by Meystel and Albus discussing research at the National Institute for Science and Technology (NIST) (Meystel and Albus, 2002).

national corps sectors was either assumed fine or treated as imperfect only through the *implicit* mechanism of low-level databases that did not allow for certain kinds of reinforcement across sectors. Communications were not treated; command, control, communications, computers, intelligence, surveillance, and reconnaissance (C^4ISR) was not considered.

It followed that relatively little U.S. analysis paid much attention to networking. There were notable exceptions associated with survivability of strategic nuclear forces and the netting of U.S. tactical air defenses, but they were definitely exceptions.[21]

Newer Approaches. Over the past decade, due partly to dramatic developments in the civil economy and partly to farsighted military officers and analysts, a great shift has been under way. It need not be elaborated in this monograph, but this shift represents a profound change in military science and decision science.

A glimpse of what was to come from the mid-1990s onward was offered by Admiral William Owens (Owens and Offley, 2000; Johnson, Owens, and Libicki, 2002). Owens' theme was suggested by his book's title, *Lifting the Fog of War*. Within DoD, the important guidance document *Joint Vision 2010* emerged in 1996, under General John Shalikashvili and Admiral Owens (Joint Staff, 1996). It emphasized such now-familiar concepts as precision engagement and information dominance.

The next wave, which continues, is often discussed under the rubric of *network-centric operations* or *network-centric warfare*. This broad approach sees information as fundamental and the network within which information flows as a core capability. Network-centric thinking has revolutionized some commercial processes and is now having profound effects within the military. Many discussions are

---

[21] The first network-centric analysis of which we happen to be aware was a 1970s study by the Institute for Defense Analyses (IDA) on bomber penetration of the Soviet Union. The IDA analysts were quite concerned that if "merely" the Soviets would learn to net their air defenses properly, as seemed straightforward technically, bomber penetration could be far more difficult than was normally assumed. Similarly, upgraded air-defense systems could be given some modicum of ballistic-missile defense capability. Fortunately, Soviet networking developed slowly.

available (see, for example, Cebrowski and Garstka, 1998; Alberts, Garstka, and Stein, 1999; National Research Council, 2000; Alberts, Garstka, Hayes, and Signori, 2001; Alberts and Hayes, 2003).

Why does network-centric operations merit a place in a monograph on decision science? Ultimately, it is because the network-centric approach *may* fundamentally change one's concept of "the system" and how it works, or can work. Thus, if we think back to the elements of the analysis process described earlier, the network-centric approach greatly affects the conceptualization of issues, the creation of alternatives, and the analysis of those alternatives. This is a frontier topic, in part because there continues to be a considerable gap between those working in the C^4ISR domain and those working on, e.g., analysis of weapons systems, platforms, and force structure.[22]

Shared Situational Awareness. One of the organizing concepts in modern decision science has come to be called, in military circles, shared situational awareness. We do not discuss it here in any depth because it is presumably well known to readers of this monograph, but this thrust, along with addressing issues such as sensemaking, is at the frontiers of decision science—not only (or even in particular) for military problems, but more generally. Good resources on the subject can be found on the website of DoD's Command and Control Research Program (CCRP). Related issues are, of course, a continuing theme at conferences such as *Enabling Technologies for Simulation Science*, within the larger SPIE conferences.

Enablers

A number of methods and tools are necessary to enable the ideas discussed above. We discuss only a few of them here, but they appear on many lists generated by workshops trying to identify cutting-edge

---

[22] One exception was an ambitious study on C^4ISR options led by Roy Evans of MITRE in the mid-1990s. Other relevant discussions exist (Alberts, Garstka, Hayes, and Signori, 2001; Starr, 2003).

issues (National Research Council, 1997, 2002; Fujimoto, Lunceford, Page, and Uhrmacher, 2002).

Multiresolution Modeling and Families of Models

It has long been recognized that decisionmakers sometimes need a broad view, without the confusing clutter of details, and they sometimes need a deep view (Bigelow and Davis, 2003). This is so for many reasons. First, any good policymaker should be expected to ask enough penetrating questions to ensure the solidity of the analysis and recommendations he is receiving. A wartime component commander may ask probing questions of even relatively junior officers as necessary to gain a sense of their preparation and their mettle. Second, policymakers who are actually thinking through alternatives and making difficult choices need to *understand* the logic of the alternatives and the logic of the assessments that compare them. That is, they need to know *why* one of the options falls apart if the budget falls below a certain number, or why another is deemed to have great growth potential. To understand may require going one, two, or multiple levels deeper. Third, the analysts preparing high-level analyses with appropriately simple models need to know whether those models (and their data) are correct, which typically requires understanding phenomena a level or two deeper.

It follows that there is great value in having *families of models* so that questions can be addressed at different levels of detail, somewhat by analogy with our having hard sciences of engineering-level formulas undergirded by thermodynamics and statistical mechanics.[23]

The theory of multiresolution modeling (also called variable-resolution modeling), which has advanced considerably in the past decade, is needed in order to construct good families of models (as well as individual models with multiple levels of resolution). Some of the work on multiresolution modeling is relatively theoretical and addresses phenomenology as well as mathematics (Davis and Bigelow, 1998).

---

[23] This idea has also been discussed to some degree by others (Krause, Christopher, and Lehman, 2003; Sisti, 2003).

Other work has looked more at various methods of metamodeling, most of which is statistical metamodeling (more in the nature of operations research or mathematics than of decision science) and some of which suggests a hybrid approach called *motivated metamodeling* (Davis and Bigelow, 2003).[24] This method urges developing low-resolution models by first using a theoretical understanding of phenomena, even if speculative, to motivate the assumed structure that is built into regressions for testing. It can have significant advantages relative to pure statistical metamodeling.

So much has happened over the past decade or so that going about building and using families of models requires substantial rethinking. Appendix B presents a first cut at such rethinking.

Agent-Based Modeling

One of the most troubling features of models used in the early decades of systems analysis and policy analysis is that they frequently did violence to the systems treated by not allowing learning, adaptation, and evolution. In the military domain, this shortcoming was described as "scripting," a practice that persists to this day and that can be made to work well only with considerable diligence on the part of the analyst. Research in the 1980s on artificial intelligence yielded a set of methods for building adaptive models, called "agents" because they often represented human beings or other living organisms. As recently as 1997, agent-based modeling in military work was discussed largely in future terms (National Research Council, 1997). In today's world, there is much less excuse for not including adaptive behaviors in military models if such adaptation is important. The science and technology of agent-based modeling is still advancing rapidly, but much already exists (Uhrmacher and Swartout, 2003; Uhrmacher, Fishwick, and Zeigler, 2001). This research deals primarily with nonmilitary applications, but the principles are general, and there are already some fascinating examples of military

---

[24] Many related papers appear in *Proceedings of SPIE* (e.g., Fall and Plotz, 2001; Haag, Chou, and Preiss, 2002; Treshansky and McGraw, 2002; Trevisani, Sisti, and Reaper, 2003); some appear in technical reports (Cassandros, 2000). These are merely examples.

applications, including the use of avatars in research-level training simulations and the use of agents to represent the behavior of individual infantrymen in difficult circumstances (Ilachinski, 2004). Recent work by the Aerospace Corporation uses the System Effectiveness Analysis Simulation (SEAS) to study Air Force issues, such as the role and effectiveness of C⁴ISR systems. There is one very short paper on the subject (Moore, Gonzales, Matonick, Pernin, and Uy, 2001). Other papers of interest include one using Bayesian-net methods to infer enemy intent (Santos, 2003), which is a part of work on multiagent distributed goal satisfaction (MADGS), and one discussing architecture for agent-based approaches (Jacobi et al., 2003).

Modular Composable Systems

Another enabler is technology for building modular, composable systems. This is important for achieving flexibility and adaptiveness: As circumstances arise, one configures a suitable system, drawing upon composable components. That, however, is easier said than done. The same is true for building models and simulations that are to be used flexibly and adaptively. Sophisticated approaches to the development of model families and multiresolution capabilities in general benefit greatly from modular designs and, in some cases, from designs that permit "composition," using modules from a variety of sources. *Model composability* is a kind of super-modularity that allows modules to be reused beyond the originator's work group—perhaps down the hall, perhaps in another branch of the same organization, perhaps in another organization altogether, and perhaps even in different fields. Advocates of composability typically have in mind great savings due to model reuse and standardization. They envision market mechanisms in which some groups develop modules, which are then offered to the world and picked up as appropriate. Such a process already exists for software (Szyperski, 2002).

Unfortunately, composing *models and simulations*, which matter so greatly to decision support, is quite a different matter from composing software modules. The central paradigm of software engineering is that modules can be viewed as black boxes that can be snapped together as long as they have the right interfaces. Models, however, are almost always imperfect representations of some segment of the real world, and they depend on assumptions that are not nearly as portable as, say, an algorithm for efficiently sorting a list or an algorithm for efficiently computing square roots. The result is that those who wish to compose a model from components must *understand* the innards of what to a software engineer would merely be black boxes. Moreover, this understanding often unveils assumptions that are inherently context-dependent.

Currently, designing models for composability is not well understood. Some progress will be made at the level of technology (e.g., modern mechanisms for incorporating and structuring metadata to explain a component and its appropriate uses). Other aspects, however, will require a deep understanding of the subtleties of simulation science and the science of modeling. One such subtlety is that models ordinarily depend upon implicit context-dependent assumptions, whereas many software components are context-independent (e.g., an algorithm for computing a square root). A recent study (Davis and Anderson, 2003) addresses the state of model composability and suggests a way for DoD to move ahead.

Decision-Support Technology

Many of the important enablers relate to the technology for decision support. We mention the following briefly: (1) evidential reasoning and abduction, (2) risk analysis, (3) debiasing techniques, and (4) collaboration technologies.

Evidential Reasoning and Abduction. Much current research in decision science relates to inferring causes or explanations from limited data. Recently, this has often been associated with the challenge of "connecting the dots," as in anticipating the terrorist attacks of September 11 from the fragmentary data that were available and, in retrospect, "should" have been valuable. Abduction is a reasoning process that proceeds from unusual observations to plausible explanations (i.e., from effects to causes) and so differs from the more familiar deduction and induction. The underlying science on such matters is being pursued in numerous fields, including law, medicine, artificial intelligence, and logic. Researchers sometimes use Bayesian nets, influence nets, and other technologies.[25]

Evidential reasoning is an abductive approach that has garnered considerable interest in the past decade (Yang and Singh, 1994). It requires decisionmakers to assign a degree of belief to each decision criterion at different levels of granularity, and it employs the Dempster-Shafer theory for combining uncertain evidence.[26] Evidential reasoning has been applied to a diverse array of engineering and business management problems and may hold promise for higher-level decision support. It has been explored in DARPA programs and others.

Risk Analysis with Bayesian Methods. Although risk analysis is a classic subject—and is one notch deeper in detail than most of this monograph—recent years have seen the emergence of some important new approaches. Modern desktop computing with tools such as Analytica and Crystal Ball now makes it possible to do Monte Carlo analyses with appropriate distribution functions and without having to make the heroic assumptions that often characterized risk-related uncertainty analysis in the classic era. On a related topic, a textbook on risk analysis (Haimes, 1998) describes a systematic way of addressing risks with long, low-probability "tails," which were classically given short shrift; it also discusses how to decompose systems properly in order to do risk analysis. This method involves the use of alternative perspectives, somewhat as in the theory of multiresolution, multiperspective modeling (MRMPM) (Zeigler, 1984; Davis and Bigelow, 1998). Although both the Morgan-Henrion and Haimes books primarily use examples from social problems, the methods are applicable to military contexts as well.

---

[25] Many related papers are published in the proceedings of the annual Conference on Uncertainty in Artificial Intelligence (UAI).

[26] The Dempster-Shafer theory is one of the principal techniques for treating uncertainty in artificial intelligence; it allows for quantifying ignorance more readily than conventional probability theory does, and it is thus especially apt for handling uncertain subjective judgments on multiple attributes (Fagin, Halpern, and Megiddo, 1990).

Methods that use Bayesian nets and influence nets were also not very feasible until the advent of modern-day high-speed desktop computing. Some discussion and citations were included in a recent study on technology for counterterrorism (National Academy of Sciences, 2002). Related work is ongoing under the sponsorship of AFRL, DARPA, and other organizations (Rosen and Smith, 1996; Wagenhals, Shin, and Levis, 2001). Santos, for example, uses Bayesian-net methods as part of adversary modeling (Santos, 2003).

Debiasing.[27] The rubric of *debiasing* refers to two ways of attempting to use decision-support systems (DSSs) to reduce bias: (1) correcting for preexisting bias and (2) not inducing new bias. The term *debiasing* is also used to mean conditioning the decisionmaker so as to reduce his propensity to judgmental biases even *without* the use of decision aids (Lipshitz, 1983), one of several purposes that war games may serve (Cohen, 2000).

Origins of Bias. Bias in decisionmaking can stem from the decisionmaker, the decision environment, or a mismatch between them. In both laboratory experiments and real-life operational decisionmaking, problems are often unfamiliar, ambiguously defined, and complicated by conflicting goals. It is not evident that "life is more charitable to people than are experimenters" in this respect (Fischhoff, 1997).[28]

In many situations DSSs may be able to debias the decision environment, making it easier to execute a given process, facilitating the use of a better process already in the decisionmaker's repertoire, or providing an information structure that works better with the process already in use (Klayman and Brown, 1993). A number of experimental debiasing systems are described in the literature, but none appear to be in active, wide use (Arnott, 2002).

---

[27] For a deeper exploration of some debiasing issues, see Appendix C.

[28] Although the heuristics and biases paradigm (HBP) is sometimes criticized for the artificiality of its experiments, it is perhaps not accidental that some of the most significant work on debiasing strategies has come from experimental psychologists conducting laboratory studies (Fischhoff, 2002).

Decision aids can also counteract the adverse effects of judg-mental biases by allowing the user to employ heuristics but warning of the likely biases, and by anticipating likely use of heuristics and providing information that offsets the effects of such use.[29] But DSS designers must recognize that decision aids can themselves *introduce* biases. For example, the manner in which decision problems are framed, such as whether outcomes are represented as gains or losses, influences the choices that are made (Kuehberger, 1998). Prospect theory holds that decisionmakers tend to be risk-averse with respect to gains but risk-loving with respect to losses (Kahneman and Tversky, 1979); it is a powerful framework for explaining risky high-level operational (Schultz, 1997) and national-strategic decisions (Levy, 2003). Decision-support systems that frame options for the user or even present, say, a neutrally phrased checklist for his consid-eration may thereby bias decisions, even if no weights are implied.

Making Conformation Biases Worse. Decision aids that incor-porate user-driven database or knowledge-base searches may reinforce confirmation biases, which stem from a decisionmaker's tendency to search for information that supports a preestablished hypothesis (Skov and Sherman, 1986) and to ignore rebutting information that may arise (Mynatt, Doherty, and Tweney, 1978). Some maintain that senior military commanders and politico-military leaders may be especially prone to such judgmental biases, due to selection bias in intellectual characteristics and to organizational forces (Dixon, 1976), but this view runs counter to contemporary findings (Wrangham, 1999).

Aids That Teach Minimax Are Biased. Operational course-of-action (COA) analysis that characterizes a COA by the nominal out-come expected if the enemy takes the worst action possible against it tilts the problem toward a "minimax" style of thinking, which is also taught in war colleges. Such thinking, however, is quite unsatisfying for an aggressive commander interested primarily in *winning*. A more balanced approach is to characterize an option by its most likely, best-

---

[29] We are not concerned here with fully automated decision tools, which are of little utility to high-level C^2 decisionmaking (Wickens and Hollands, 1999).

case, and worst-case outcomes (Davis, 2003b) and then identify the circumstances that would enhance the likelihood of the best-case outcome and reduce the likelihood of the worst case.

Debiasing Can Be Counterproductive Because of Stale Information. Caution should be exercised in assuming that a particular theoretical bias actually exists and creates problems in an operational environment. Moreover, efforts to preclude such biases, motivated by the general literature, can be counterproductive. For example, a casual reading of the literature might suggest that the bias of base-rate neglect can be easily and properly removed by DSSs. Upon consideration, however, we realize that many judgments require the decisionmaker to *combine* information about a more-or-less stable average incidence of some class of events (the "base rate") with specific information about a member of that class. A commander might know, for instance, that an enemy has only rarely been found to collocate military communications operations in hospitals, but he has fresh intelligence that encrypted radio transmissions are issuing from a particular hospital. How should he balance the old base-rate information with the new information? It seems unlikely to us that a generic DSS algorithm would resolve that dilemma.

Using Frequency Depictions to Assist in Bayesian Reasoning. Classical decision theory dictates, by Bayes' law, that prior probabilities inform the interpretation of new information, but many studies have shown that even experts given familiar problems are not intuitively Bayesian. A famous medical-school experiment illustrates this. When told that a disease is present in 0.1 percent of the population and that the probability of a false-positive result on a test for the disease is 0.05, nearly half of the subjects estimated that a randomly selected person who tests positive has a 95 percent chance of having the disease. The reader should quickly make his or her own estimate before reading on.

Fewer than 20 percent of those tested offered an estimate in the neighborhood of the correct value of 2 percent (Casscells, Schoenberger, and Grayboys, 1978). When the medical-school experiment was replicated some years later, the control group presented with the probabilistic problem formulation performed as poorly as those in the original experiment did, but the subjects given a frequentist formulation did not ignore the Bayesian prior and estimated the result correctly (Cosmides and Tooby, 1996). A frequentist depiction might say that in 10,000 patients, about 500 will falsely test positive and 50 will actually have the disease (e.g., cancer). If that is clearer than the first statement, consider the pictorial depiction in Figure 4.4, which shows clearly that the fraction of positives corresponding to real cancer patients is very small. Indeed, it is 10/510, or about 0.02, as mentioned above. In this and other cases, both a frequentist depiction and a visual version thereof can do a lot to improve the quality of judgment (Gigerenzer and Selten, 2002). This is of interest because some of today's high-level DSSs rely on prob-

Figure 4.4
Graphical Depiction of High False-Positive Rates

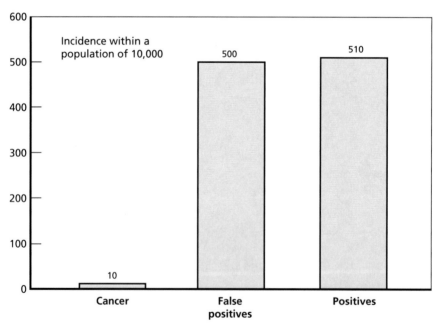

abilistic formulations and might be better served by a shift to frequentist depictions.[30]

But the Frequentist Approach Can also Cause Problems. Unfortunately, there are no panaceas, and the alleged general superiority of the frequentist depiction is hotly disputed, on both methodological and theoretical grounds (Evans, Handley, Perham, Over, and Thompson, 2000). Indeed, the countervailing studies contend that decisionmakers presented with frequentist data ignore diagnostic evidence and overweight the base rate. As an example related to the research findings, if a commander were told that "you'd expect to find chemical weapons in a bunker of that sort two times out of ten," the syntax may improperly suggest that the estimate is empirically well rooted, when in fact it merely represents a subjective estimate by intelligence officers.

Some recent research addresses the issue of which statistical format is preferred in different situations (Brase, 2002). Other studies find that formulations such as "the odds are one to four against finding chemical weapons in that bunker" are the most readily understood (Heuer, 1999). Still other investigators maintain that biases that appear to reflect insufficient reaction to new evidence may in fact serve the decisionmaker well in the face of real-world changes affecting the reliability or significance of evidence (Cohen, 1993). In short, framing likelihoods as probabilities or frequencies can influence decisionmaker judgments and the extent to which they approximate Bayesian reasoning, but more research is required to derive useful prescriptions for decision support. The potential for DSS is high, but the prescriptions remain ambiguous. Koehler (1996) presents a good discussion of how complex the issue is but also suggests useful principles for making sense of the conflicting literature. The suggestions reflect appropriate skepticism for uncritical acceptance of alleged base rates while also summarizing the methods that can be used to encourage paying attention to base rates.

---

[30] An example is the CAESAR II/COA system used in war games (Heacox, Quinn, Kelly, and Gwynne, 2002)

Collaboration Technologies. One technological consideration in several of the techniques discussed above is the quality of virtual collaboration. Advances have occurred steadily for more than two decades, and virtual collaboration, to include web-based modeling and simulation, is increasing. There are issues, however, that arise in virtual, rather than face-to-face collaboration. These have been reviewed recently (Wainfan and Davis, 2004). There are also difficult challenges in envisioning the entire virtual environment and the requirements for information exchange that go with it (McQuay, 2003).

Cutting-edge work in collaborative discussion, reasoning, and decision is ongoing in a number of companies, including SRI International, which has the HARP (Human Augmenting Reasoning Through Patterning) program, the tools of which encourage multiple perspectives and evidential reasoning. One such tool is SEAS (Structured Evidential Argumentation System). As in other current-day approaches to decision support, there is great emphasis on maintaining alternative hypotheses and seeking decisions that are robust under uncertainty.

Tools for effective networking and collaboration are important in everyday life, as demonstrated by countless teenagers who multitask every night as they do homework, participate in chat rooms, and talk on cell phones (Roberts, Foehr, and Rideout, 2005). Such tools are also important for decision support. In the most recent Gulf war, U.S. military C^2 was highly distributed, with subordinate commanders even being in separate countries. Joint staffs worked on complex problems such as targeting, retargeting, and battle-damage assessment, using collaborative tools. This was but the beginning of a dramatic evolution in the years ahead. Although commanders are already well served with videoconferencing, implications of distributed networks for higher-level decision support are not as yet well understood. Since one recurring recommendation for support of decision-makers is assuring that they "reach out" to experts and provocative thinkers wherever they may be, in order to broaden their recognition of factors and possibilities, it is also important to have tools to help in doing so. The Wainfan-Davis study (2004) reminds us that this may not be trivial and that science can help.

CHAPTER FIVE

The Research Frontier: Reconciling Analytic and Intuitive Considerations

Introduction

As indicated in Chapter Two, a consensus is forming on how humans make decisions, but major conflicts persist about how humans *should* make decisions and, by extension, how human decisionmaking can be improved, i.e., what the prescription should be. This chapter moves toward a synthesis on the prescriptive issues.

Comparing Decisionmaking Paradigms

The evolution of decisionmaking theory can be envisioned as a slow, steady retreat from the rational-choice model (RCM), as shown schematically in Figure 5.1. The classic notion (sometimes implicit) was that RCM often applied to both actual and desired behavior, which fit well with economic theory of the time. The retreat began with Simon's concept of bounded rationality (Simon, 1982b), which emphasized constraints of time, resources, and cognitive capacity. These constraints force decisionmakers to construct a simplified mental model of the world. Although decisionmakers may act rationally within this model, the results are not necessarily rational by classic standards.

Bounded rationality was resisted by many because it was unclear how one could operationalize it, whereas one could do straightforward (and sometimes elegant) mathematics with RCM. Nonetheless, facts are stubborn, and the concept is today well accepted. However, the mantle of bounded rationality is now claimed by those working

Figure 5.1
Evolution of Decision Theory

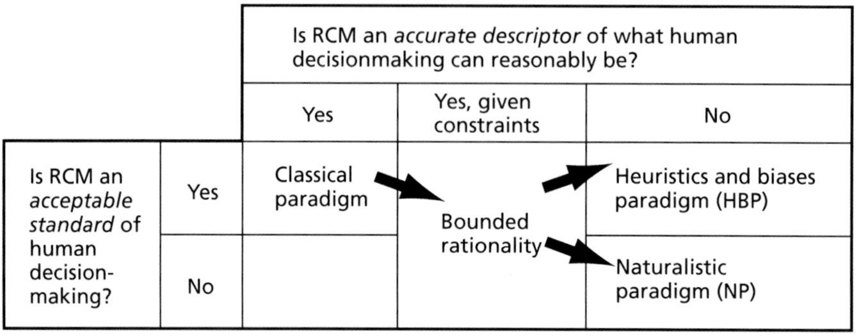

		Is RCM an *accurate descriptor* of what human decisionmaking can reasonably be?		
		Yes	Yes, given constraints	No
Is RCM an *acceptable standard* of human decision-making?	Yes	Classical paradigm		Heuristics and biases paradigm (HBP)
			Bounded rationality	
	No			Naturalistic paradigm (NP)

RAND *MG360-5.1*

under two very different paradigms, the heuristics and biases paradigm (HBP) and the naturalistic paradigm (NP), both of which were discussed in Chapter Two.

At the distinct risk of oversimplification, it can be said that those pursuing HBP have emphasized that, because of a built-in tendency to use heuristics, humans often do not follow RCM, even when time and effort requirements are not issues (Tversky and Kahneman, 1974). By using RCM as a baseline for comparison, HBP researchers effectively suggested that decisions *should* be made by RCM, albeit constrained by bounded rationality. In Figure 5.1, then, HBP suggests that RCM is not descriptively accurate, but that it is the appropriate standard. In contrast, adherents of NP argue that RCM is often neither descriptive nor desirable!

Table 5.1 presents a generalized comparison of HBP and NP. Heuristics and biases research typically is conducted in a laboratory setting: Research subjects are presented with a task and asked to provide a choice, judgment, preference, or estimate. Often these tasks have a "right" answer, that is, a mathematically precise estimate or a normatively dominant choice. The goal of HBP research is to measure systematic deviations of subjects' answers from the normative answers, with the hope that these deviations will provide insights into the way the mind structures decisions.

Table 5.1
Comparing the Heuristics and Biases and Naturalistic Paradigms

Parameter	Heuristics and Biases (HBP)	Naturalistic (NP)
Approach		
Environment	Laboratory	The field
Subjects	All types	Experts
Method	Choice elicitation	Choice observation
Measure	Deviation from RCM	Success of strategies
Descriptive Model		
Situation assessment	Heuristics	Pattern matching and story building
Risk accounting	Heuristics	Mental simulation
Strategy selection	Rule-based, breadth-first	Intuitive, depth-first
Source of error	Decisionmaker	Environment
View of Normative Models		
Rational choice	Desirable	Potentially burdensome
Intuition/expertise	Potentially misleading	Key to human success
View of Decision Support		
Role of decision support[a]	Check decisionmaker	Support decisionmaker style
Role of training	Develop statistical skills	Develop expertise

[a] This oversimplifies. For example, NP recognizes the value of framing and displaying information in order to reduce bias, as in medicine (Patel, Kaufman, and Arocha, 2002). More generally, the sharp differences blur upon closer inspection (Kahneman and Tversky, 1996).

NP research takes a decidedly different approach: Decision-making is observed in a "real-world" setting, complete with time pressure, uncertainty, ill-defined goals, high personal stakes, multiple actors, and dynamic environments (Lipshitz, Klein, Orasanu, and Salas, 2001). Moreover, NP research tends to measure the decision-making strategies of experts acting in the domain of their expertise. The goal of this research is to use real-world observation to better understand real-world decisionmaking, with the hope that expert strategies hold prescriptive value for improving decisionmaking in general.

Even as *descriptive* models, the two approaches are quite different. While HBP researchers often assume a breadth-first selection process with a series of rule-based decisions, NP observes depth-first processes that make choices quickly and intuitively (Klein, 1998). In NP, the expert first attempts to match the current situation to similar situations in the past. If a match is found, the decisionmaker engages in "recognition-primed decisionmaking" and applies the knowledge from the earlier match to generate a solution to the present situation. If a match cannot be retrieved, the decisionmaker engages in explanation-based reasoning, trying to assess the situation based on the evidence at hand. To gauge risk, the expert then mentally simulates the potential course of action, to imagine whether it will work and to envision any adverse consequences. Rather than blaming errors on faulty reasoning, as is done in HBP, mistakes are attributed to such factors as "poor training or dysfunctional organizational demands, or flawed design of a human-computer interface" (Lipshitz, Klein, Orasanu, and Salas, 2001).

The Value of Synthesis

Table 5.1 suggests that there is a chasm between the two schools, and, as mentioned in Chapter Two, much ink has been spilled over the disagreements between them. Our own view is that the differences can be both exaggerated and understated. As we discuss below, citing many thoughtful studies, some of the differences disappear under scrutiny. This said, it would be difficult to overstate the significance of the attitudinal differences and their effects on practical issues such as how people are educated, trained, and allegedly helped by DSSs. In referring to the need for synthesis, we have much more in mind than merely itemizing carefully the points on which the two schools do and do not agree technically. We believe that pursuing synthesis could have profound effects on the approach to decision support. With this in mind, let us first note how some of the gap is less real than is sometimes claimed and then turn to the more difficult issues and their implications for decision support.

Elements of Synthesis

More than two decades ago, it was observed that normative and descriptive theories of decisionmaking were converging and that it was counterproductive to insist on the distinction (Kahan and Rapoport, 1984). We agree, despite the long tradition of that distinction.

One way to blur the distinction is to use "dual-process theories," on which a recent review is available (Stanovich and West, 2002). This approach explains differing human responses to experiments in terms of two systems. System 1 is intuitive and fast, using heuristics to make effort-minimizing decisions about the world. These shortcuts are often useful, but they can lead to systematic deviations from rational norms. System 2, conversely, is slow, effortful, and rule-based. It can handle more-deliberative decisions, and it also serves as a check for when intuitive decisions appear to violate statistical norms. Error can be considered a failure of both cognitive systems: System 1 for generating the erroneous decision, and System 2 for failing to "notice" the error. Whether one is referring to how humans *do* make decisions or how they *should* make them, the existence of both systems or modes makes sense and is supported by research.

One paper (Eisenhardt and Zbaracki, 1992) reviewed numerous case studies of mid- to high-level strategic decisionmakers to characterize the decision processes used and found that many decisionmakers employ different techniques, depending on the circumstances of the decision problem or the decision environment. The recently propounded theory of poliheuristic decisionmaking is gaining currency in foreign-policy analysis (Dacey and Carlson, 2004). Much like proponents of the dual-process theories that have emerged from the cognitive and behavioral sciences, political scientists contend that decisionmakers first employ holistic decision processes (including interpretive stories) to eliminate politically unacceptable alternatives and then employ a classically analytic decision procedure to select from the remaining set of acceptable alternatives. This theory has been tested in experiments with high-ranking Air Force officers playing the roles of senior foreign-policy and national-security decisionmakers (Mintz, 2004).

In summary, humans are willing and able to use processes associated with intuition, pattern recognition, and flowing adaptation, as well as processes associated with approximations to rational choice, depending on the circumstances.

The gap between the HBP and NP schools is wider concerning how humans *should* decide and how best to help them decide well. Attempts to capture HBP and NP within a single normative framework have mostly been at a high level of abstraction (Samuels, Stich, and Bishop, 2002). However, at least one study (Payne, Bettman, and Johnson, 1993) took a lower-level view, examining consumer decisionmaking behavior, and found a contingent mix of analytic and intuitive decision processes. The authors provided recommendations for improving decisionmaking, by recognizing which process is the most apt in given circumstances and by changing the decision *environment* so as to make a chosen decision process more successful. Furthermore, they contended that "intelligent, adaptive decision support systems appear to be a promising idea" (p. 233) but noted that differences in personality and decision tasks pose a daunting challenge to DSS designers.

Tarter and Hoy cast an even wider net and propounded a "contingency theory" of decisionmaking, which incorporates various administrative and political models as well as classical and intuitive individual-level models (Tarter and Hoy, 1998). They were appropriately cautious in stipulating which method is best suited to which circumstances.

From a DSS-centric perspective, one author (Silverman, 1994) bravely essayed a "unified decision approach" to synthesize expert system and mathematical decision theories. The former largely correspond to intuitive decisionmaking theories; the latter, to constrained RCM.

It seems, then, that the time is ripe for synthesis and that research is emerging to support it: Humans make decisions differently, depending on circumstances, and they *should* make decisions differently, depending on circumstances. Perhaps this is a moment for the proverbial "Duh!," but the boundary lines drawn in academic research sometimes obscure this point.

With this background, let us now begin the cautious move in the direction of a *practical* synthesis, one that goes beyond theoretical reconciliation and produces actionable recommendations for decision support. We confront two major issues: (1) improving automated decision support, and (2) balancing what can be termed *cold* and *story-based* decision support.

Improving Automated Decision Support

Challenges

At first blush, it seems that the naturalistic and rationalistic paradigms hold irreconcilable views on the role of computerized decision support. The difficulty is highlighted by an example:

> The DSS-1 [a decision-support system for fighter pilots] had a comparison-to-norms module, which provided color-coded squares to show how well a set of critical parameters [e.g., speed, altitude] for the selected track fit a template for known threats [good fit, questionable fit, or poor fit] and support pattern matching. This module was not well liked and was not used as had been intended. It was, therefore, dropped from the DSS-2 (Morrison, Kelly, Moore, and Hutchins, 2000).

An NP adherent would wholeheartedly endorse this removal. The comparison-to-norms module, rather than aiding the pilot's decision, attempted to supplant his intuitive skill at pattern matching by dictating a measure of typicality using an obscure algorithm. Furthermore, the fact that it was not liked and had not been used as intended revealed poor "cognitive ergonomics"—a mismatch with the thinking style of the pilot.

An HBP advocate would strongly disagree with this assessment. The comparison-to-norms module, while perhaps not designed optimally, was an important graphical representation of the typicality of a reference class—a crucial step in correcting for the tendency to overlook regression-to-the-mean in making intuitive estimates. The fact that the module had not been liked or used properly was not a normative issue but an operational one. If anything, the pilots' inability or unwillingness to compare the current situation to norms revealed a dangerous gap in their intuitive reasoning.

Who is right? Normatively, both paradigms seem to fall short. It does little good to include a decision aid that is ignored and disliked; after all, "an unused decision aid is a worthless decision aid" (Kaplan, Reneau, and Whitecotton, 2001). On the other hand, an unused decision aid might be valuable if decisionmakers would learn how to use it. This suggests a two-pronged approach to improving automated decision tools. Not only should the tools be made more user-friendly (as recommended by NP), the decisionmaker should be made more mathematically sophisticated (as recommended by HBP) in order to be able to appreciate the value of the tools. The goal, therefore, is to optimize the fit between a decisionmaker and a potentially valuable decision tool—and to have the decisionmaker appreciate that fit, consciously or not—recognizing that *both* can be improved.

Perhaps the overriding desideratum is that the decisionmaker have the correct level of *trust* in his decision aids; one proposed framework consists of (1) appropriate trust—information is good and the user trusts it, (2) false trust—information is poor and the user trusts it, (3) false distrust—information is good and the user distrusts it, and (4) appropriate distrust—information is poor and the user distrusts it (Muir and Moray, 1984).

"Trust" has been discussed as a social construct and as a relationship between humans and automated systems (Lee and See, 2004); it is also discussed in one study on aided adversarial decisionmaking (Llinas, Bisantz, Drury, Song, and Jian, 1998). Cohen argues for a situation-specific trust model:

> The problem of decision aid acceptance is neither undertrust nor overtrust as such, but inappropriate trust: a failure to understand or properly evaluate the conditions affecting good and bad aid performance. To the extent that decision aid acceptance has foundered on the issue of trust, training deserves some of the responsibility. Training focuses on inputting required information, changing modes, and reading outputs. Such training inadvertently reinforces the misconception that trust must be an

invariant stance, to accept or reject an aid as a whole. There has been little effort to teach skills for evaluating an aid's performance in real time, and training strategies for interacting with the aid based on that evaluation (Cohen, 2002, p. 1).

Concrete Suggestions for Design of Decision Support

Current decision science recommends a number of ways to increase the usage and trustworthiness of decision tools by improving the tools themselves and the users' interactions:

- **Tool Design Features**
  - *Allow personalization.* Decisionmakers rate a tool as more usable when they can customize certain features, such as window size and chart scale (Morrison, Kelly, Moore, and Hutchins, 2000). They also may reject a tool that they feel compromises their "art" (Arkes, Dawes, and Christensen, 1986).
  - *Use graphical interfaces.* Decisionmakers also rate graphical tools as more trustworthy than text-based modules (Bisantz et al., 2000). However, there may be an interaction with complexity; that is, graphical interfaces are more appropriate for complex tasks, while text-based interfaces are sometimes more appropriate for simple tasks (Speier and Morris, 2003).
  - *Maintain interactivity.* Decisionmakers prefer an interactive tool to a noninteractive tool, even when they perform better with the latter (Kaplan, Reneau, and Whitecotton, 2001). Of course, this changes if interactivity requirements are so severe as to be burdensome (Morrison, Kelly, Moore, and Hutchins, 2000).
  - *Limit preprocessing of data.* Decisionmakers prefer decision-support calculations (such as ranking alternatives) that can easily be linked to concepts in the "hard data." They should also have access to all of the underlying data used by the decision tool (Morrison, Kelly, Moore, and Hutchins, 2000).

- **Decision Tool/User Interaction**
  - *Explain the tool's reasoning system.* Explanations of the tool's principles and underlying processes can assure (or ultimately convince) the user that its reasoning is logical and its conclusions sound, relevant, and useful (Irandoust, 2002). A user who finds that a tool has made an error may distrust other, even previously reliable, decision aids, unless the error is explained (Dzindolet, Peterson, Pomranky, Pierce, and Beck, 2003).
  - *Increase early user involvement.* Decisionmakers will rely more on a decision tool when they have used it during training. Reliance will also increase if the decisionmaker was involved in the original development of the decision tool (Kaplan, Reneau, and Whitecotton, 2001).
  - *Control validity information.* When decisionmakers are told how accurate a decision tool is, they will overestimate their own accuracy and rely less on the tool (Arkes, Dawes, and Christensen, 1986). Therefore, this validity information should be either withheld or presented along with information on the decisionmakers' personal accuracy (Kaplan, Reneau, and Whitecotton, 2001).

  As we noted in the discussion of debiasing in Chapter Four, decision science also points to several simple ways of increasing the mathematical sophistication of the decisionmakers using these automated tools:

  - *Teach decisionmakers about decisionmaking biases* and the situations in which they might be vulnerable to them (Schultz, 1997).
  - *Expose decisionmakers to statistical concepts* and instruct them on how and when to "think like statisticians" (Nisbett, Krantz, Jepson, and Fong, 1982). Admittedly, there are doubts about the feasibility of this approach, which we share. As Nobel Laureate Richard Thaler noted ruefully in a lecture that one of the present authors (Davis) attended, even serious students who did well in a course devoted to this goal made

the same classic errors when retested a year or two later, suggesting that human shortcomings in this regard are wired in and can be overcome only with extreme difficulty.

- *Show base rates and frequencies graphically* (Gigerenzer and Selten, 2002; Stone et al., 2003). One does not have to buy into the frequentist school's views (e.g., those of Gigerenzer) to recognize that graphical presentations are often more cognitively effective than mathematical expressions are.

- *Use decision tools to display typicality information, alternative hypotheses, and disconfirming evidence* (Morrison, Kelly, Moore, and Hutchins, 2000). If generating alternatives is perceived as easy, encouraging people to consider alternatives reduces many biases not only in the domain of the experiment but in unrelated domains as well (Hirt, Kardes, and Markman, 2004).

Balancing Cold and Story-Based Decision Support

A second critical issue in higher-level decision support is that of balancing what can be termed *cold analysis*—numbers, facts, and figures—with *story-based analysis* that relies on context, past experience, and narrative impact. HBP proponents would argue that the former should be emphasized at the expense of the latter; indeed, attempts by decisionmakers to consider information external to the experimental frame (such as the ease of visualizing a certain outcome) or to exclude relevant data (such as base rates) from consideration are generally considered prima facie evidence of bias. Naturalistic research, on the other hand, emphasizes the importance of stories in tying hard data to the real world.

While the term *story* appears often in decision science, especially in the naturalistic literature, it is somewhat confusingly used to describe two different phenomena: *Persuasion stories* are arguments or observations that sway a decisionmaker toward a specific course of action. They can take many forms, including anecdotes, analogies, past experiences, gut feelings, moral arguments, and pure conjecture.

For example, an anecdote about a fighter pilot mistakenly targeting a commercial airliner might sway an air-defense officer from advocating a shootdown in an ambiguous situation. Historical analogies are often used, cynically or in earnest, to frame decision situations so as to compel particular policy decisions (Khong, 1992). Even so, ostensibly similar analogies can yield divergent policy prescriptions (e.g., "Iraq is just like Vietnam so we should get out now" versus "Iraq is just like Vietnam so we need to show resolve"). *Interpretive stories* are explanations that the decisionmaker uses to tie together observation, opinion, and intuition. For example, a reluctant air-defense officer might construct the story that his ambiguous radar track is nothing more than a friendly pilot who has forgotten to turn on the IFF (identify friend or foe) system. The interpretive story serves as the decisionmaker's "best guess" of what is going on and therefore drives the course of action that is eventually taken.

Stories are employed to integrate (1) facts or information from the current situation, (2) knowledge about similar situations, and (3) generic expectations about what makes a complete story, such as believing that people do what they do for a reason (Klein, 1998). In essence, then, decisionmaking is a process that uses cold analysis and persuasion stories to generate an interpretive story, which in turn generates action. The role of stories, for both persuasion and interpretation, has been extensively studied only in jury decisionmaking (Hastie and Pennington, 2000) and in attorneys' legal argumentation (Verheij, 2001). The practical issue for decision support is that of how large a role persuasion stories should play in this process. A secondary concern is how persuasion stories, if deemed appropriate, are best conveyed to decisionmakers?

The crux of this second normative synthesis is that *the proper balance between stories and cold analysis depends on the characteristics of the decision being faced, the decision environment, and the decisionmaker.* These characteristics include decision class, time pressure, group homogeneity, level of data-quality information, level of ambiguity, irreversibility, and emotional distress.

Decision Characteristics

Decision Class. Two papers thirty-some years apart (Bormann, 1969; Gouran, 2003) observed that the question at the root of a specific decision can be classified as one of fact, of value, or of policy. Returning to the example of the air-defense officer looking at an ambiguous radar track, if he knew what the track actually represented, then the fact-based decision would be obvious: shoot the enemy, spare the friend. By contrast, for defense planners facing a resources-constrained choice between two aircraft proposed for development, the decision is fully value-based; all facts are known, but the decision remains, since it is now rooted in a tradeoff of conflicting preferences. Finally, many operational decision situations—which can be called policy-based—are richer and more complex than these examples, in that they involve both factual uncertainty and a difficult conflict of values.

Holding situation-specific characteristics equal, a fact-based decision regards reaching "the truth" as paramount. Consequently, cold analysis and stories should be aligned against each other through iterative correction and calibration. New data should challenge the applicability of influential stories; new stories should challenge the reliability of influential data.

On the other hand, the priority of value-based decisions is to make an accurate and complete comparison. To do this optimally, all relevant factors should be catalogued and compared in what is, essentially, the rational choice method (even naturalistic researchers recognize its usefulness in such situations (Klein, 1998)). While persuasion stories may be useful in an exploratory role—highlighting additional factors to be included in an analytical model—these decisions usually require a process heavy in cold analysis.

Finally, policy-based decisions with multiple levels of uncertainty should ideally select the strategy option that is most robust and adaptive given uncertainties and value structure (Davis, 2002a; Lempert, 2002). This suggests a more complex value calculation that factors in the direct costs of a specific course of action and the indirect costs of being wrong. The proper calibration of cold processes and stories will depend strongly on these other decision characteristics.

Level of Ambiguity. When decisionmakers use structured-decisionmaking analysis, they tend to exclude ambiguous factors that are not easily measurable (van Dijk and Zeelenberg, 2003). Persuasion stories may serve a vital role in putting these factors back into consideration if they were overlooked (Luce and Raiffa, 1989; Frostic, Lewis, and Bowie, 1993).

Decision-Environment Characteristics

Time Pressure. When a decision must be made under extreme time pressure, cold analysis may require too much time. Stories can impart much more contextual information than they explicitly state. If the storyteller and the audience share common assumptions, this can be an efficient way of quickly relating a large quantity of information—if not, then assuming a common understanding of the context may be quite risky (Gershon and Eick, 1995). Automated decision aids can help, but often a decision must be made before all factors have been considered. In these cases, stories (especially comparisons to past experience and gut feelings) may be valuable in preventing paralysis. Whether a story is best related as a written or a graphical narrative depends on the particular cognitive characteristics of the audience, as well as on the content of the story (Wojtkowski and Wojtkowski, 2002).

Level of Data-Quality Information. Data-quality information (DQI) gauges the accuracy and reliability of in-hand data. If DQI is unavailable or there is reason to believe that the data being analyzed are suspect, an overreliance on cold analysis will lead to false precision and a skewed interpretive story. In these cases, persuasion stories (e.g., those involving past experience) should assume greater importance.

Irreversibility. In general, NP advocates a "try-and-adapt" approach to making decisions, while rational norms imply a careful first search for the "best" option. However, in some decisions, there is no room for adaptation—either the missile is fired or it is not. In these cases, persuasion stories should be examined critically, so that they do not lead to an irreversible error (note that this may cause the air-defense officer to think twice about relying on stories due to time pressure).

Decisionmaker Characteristics

Group Homogeneity. If a decisionmaker receives support from a group of individuals with similar expertise, life experiences, worldviews, and goals, their persuasion stories may systematically neglect to cover an important area of the decision and thus systematically bias the interpretive story. In general, the role of persuasion stories should be underweighted in such groups.

Level of Emotional Distress. A long line of decision research has demonstrated that desperate or upset decisionmakers take riskier actions than their calmer or happier counterparts do (Mellers, Schwartz, and Cooke, 1998). It seems plausible that such decisionmakers would be especially vulnerable to "pie in the sky" stories that promise great rewards or simply a way out of a bad situation. During emotionally trying times, decisionmakers should rely less on stories and more on cold analysis.

General Recommendations

Building from the research, we offer several general recommendations for improving this dimension of decision support:

- Put checks and balances on persuasion stories;
- Create diverse decisionmaking groups;
- Know the limitations of advice;
- Institutionalize skepticism;
- Formalize the use of alternative models, including adversary models, in doctrine.

Some of these are offered as hypotheses that should be subjected to empirical testing. We now address each of them in turn.

Put checks and balances on persuasion stories. A good story is "coherent, informative, persuasive, memorable, emotionally salient, and/or interesting" (Graesser, Olde, and Klettke, 2002). Armed with these strengths, a good story can fundamentally alter the way decisionmakers view a problem. Consequently, storytelling should never be a one-sided exercise. Stories "rooting for" one outcome of a decision should be balanced, whenever possible, by stories supporting the opposite outcome (e.g., vivid anecdotes of what has gone wrong should accompany stories of what has gone right, and vice versa). Competing stories will prompt decisionmakers to evaluate the relative typicality or applicability of each, which is a crucial step in controlling the stories' influence. If possible, stories should be evaluated against measurable data (e.g., to measure the actual typicality of a persuasion anecdote).

Create diverse decisionmaking groups. As suggested above, decisionmakers should ideally receive decision support from people with varying expertise, life experiences, worldviews, and goals. To the extent that people generate persuasion stories from these intangible factors, this diversity will create a rich set of competing stories, with the benefits outlined above. Diversity of opinion can also reduce the dangers of overconfidence and groupthink (Janis, 1982).

Know the limitations of advice. At the same time, seeking a diverse set of advice has its own dangers. Decision research has identified a "confidence heuristic," by which decisionmakers judge their most confident advisor as the one most likely to be correct, even when that confidence is misplaced (Price and Stone, 2004). Equally problematic, people who consider themselves highly knowledgeable about a subject are likely to discount valuable advice altogether (Yaniv, 2004) and to ignore DQI when it is available (Fisher, Chengalur-Smith, and Ballou, 2003). Once again, we might systematize the process in order to give equal scrutiny to each opinion, and we might possibly try to educate decisionmakers about their potential biases.

Institutionalize skepticism. As shown in the examples above, a single set of circumstances can produce perfectly reasonable but completely opposite interpretations. There has been broad consensus within HBP and NP on the existence of a "belief bias"—that once a decisionmaker forms an interpretive story, he or she will process all subsequent observations within that interpretive filter, noticing the data that support the earlier interpretation and discarding the data that do not. To control for this bias, it would seem that decisionmakers on the ground should use (at least informally) something like the "basis for assessment" module designed for fighter pilots (Morrison, Kelly, Moore, and Hutchins, 2000), in which the evidence for and against each of several possible interpretive stories is tabulated and compared. Acceptance, however, will depend critically upon quality of implementation. Other methods for institutionalizing skepticism include bringing new faces into the process midstream and using devil's advocates. The latter method has not proven effective in the past, but this may be because people become tarred with the contrary interpretation and are then discounted personally. Perhaps rotating the responsibility for presenting contrary interpretations would improve results.

Formalize the use of alternative models in doctrine. Alternative adversary models, for example, are an impersonal but potentially effective way of opening minds (Davis, 2002b; Kulick and Davis, 2003b).

Despite all the "dangers" of persuasion stories highlighted above, these stories are nevertheless a crucial part of decisionmaking, as is evident from case histories of national-security decisionmaking. Total reliance on either cold analysis or stories alone can easily lead to significant and systematic error. Hybrid approaches are being studied in ongoing RAND research.

CHAPTER SIX

Conclusions

This monograph (including its appendices) provides a highly selective review of decision science developed with the Air Force Research Laboratory in mind. Some highlights follow that may be relevant to AFRL's research agenda.

The Decisionmaking Component

Modern decision science embraces a far greater understanding than was previously available of how individuals and groups go about decisionmaking, the problems to which they are subject, and the issues that should be borne in mind when developing decision support. Not very long ago, much of the emphasis here was on "debiasing" decisions in ways suggested by the heuristics and biases school associated with Kahneman and Tversky. More recently, however, a conflicting paradigm has arisen under the rubric of naturalistic decisionmaking. Based on our review, we conclude the following:

- A synthesis should be developed between the two schools, because both have much to offer.
- Some of this synthesis can be achieved by knowing the circumstances under which to use the rational-analytic paradigm, rather than, say, the "primed pattern recognition" often mentioned in naturalistic decisionmaking. Real-time operations will often depend on experts acting intuitively, on the basis of internalized

knowledge. But this internalized knowledge should, we presume, be created in part by highly structured exposure to situations and dilemmas. The success stories of naturalistic research are primarily associated with *experts* following their intuition. Moreover, even being an expert is not enough, as the disastrous errors of many famous commanders throughout history should remind us. "Highly structured exposure," then, should address a wide range of circumstances.

- How naturalistic principles should be taken into account when supporting high-level decisionmaking associated with, say, peacetime planning, development of war plans, or political-military crisis management (as distinct from the real-time actions of a pilot) is a cutting-edge issue. We presented some ideas and recommendations on this matter in Chapter Five, but the issue is not yet well understood. Both theoretical and empirical research are badly needed, research that cuts across the academic "schools" to solve problems.

The Analysis Component

Several themes should be kept in mind in developing decision-support systems and their underlying research base. These include (1) the need to *understand* the target system; (2) the need to deal effectively with uncertainty, which is often massive; and (3) the need to interact with the user, and iterate.

It follows that great emphasis should also be placed on

- Multifaceted, multilayered understanding of relevant systems and their phenomena, both "hard" and "soft";
- Planning for adaptiveness and, as part of that, the search for strategies that are flexible, adaptive, and robust;
- Using the constructs of complex adaptive system (CAS) theory to structure inquiry.

These principles have numerous implications for research, methods, and tools. They imply the need to emphasize, e.g., exploratory analysis, multiresolution modeling, families of models, and new types of search tools concerned not with optimization but with the criteria of flexibility, adaptiveness, and robustness. Where meaningful prediction and optimization are feasible, related solutions should fall out as special cases, but this will be the exception rather than the rule in much work. Internalizing this change of paradigm is of fundamental importance to the future of decision-support systems.

Developing meaningful models and simulations to support such work will require extensive agent-based modeling *and* new concepts for using such models analytically, despite the fact that their behaviors are not as stable and easy to understand as are those of more-traditional models. In warfare, the sides' learning and adapting is fundamental, not something on the margin. A variety of adversary-modeling techniques need to be pursued, including those using Bayesian-net methods and those taking a more top-down approach with hierarchical decision tables.

Because constructing model families will require dealing with heterogeneity of formalism, representation, and the like, tools will be needed to assist in doing so.

Interaction and iteration are, in practice, associated with virtual organizations and virtual forms of communication. Related phenomena need to be understood in depth so that technology and methods can be designed to achieve high performance with minimal errors of the sort that arise in virtual work.

Both the need to achieve a deep understanding and the need to deal effectively with uncertainty through flexibility, adaptiveness, and robustness yield a need for great emphasis on C^2 and networking. Much effort is currently being directed to these matters, but it is possible, and perhaps likely, that an entirely new generation of models and simulations will be needed if military analysis and related decision support are to fully reflect and exploit the potential of ubiquitous networking.

Such new-generation models may need architectures very different from those of past models, in which C^2 was a mere support function and networking was largely omitted except in old-fashioned modeling of point-to-point communications.

Debiasing an Air Campaign[1]

Let us consider a concrete illustration of the role of judgmental biases in operational DSSs: a notional campaign and a commander charged with operational decisions, in this case, the Joint Force Air Component Commander (JFACC) producing the master air-attack plan (MAAP) and daily air tasking orders (ATOs) (U.S. Air Force, 1994). We pose plausible circumstances for representative judgmental biases within a narrative of this campaign and tasks and consider the possible role of DSS. This thought experiment does not reflect any actual DSS in current use or development; many of those are no doubt well ahead of our thinking in these regards. Rather, it entails a caricature of the JFACC's proneness to biased judgment.

We use the judgmental bias taxonomy from Chapter Two; the narrative illustrates one bias from each category:

- Memory biases: most fundamental, concern storage and recall of information;
- Naïve statistical biases: nonprobabilistic information processing;
- Confidence biases: excessive confidence in own judgment and decisionmaking skill;
- Adjustment biases: undue attachment to initial assumptions;
- Presentation biases: cognitive effects of how information is perceived and initially processed;

---

[1] This appendix is excerpted from a conference paper (Kulick and Davis, 2003a).

- Choice biases: highest level of abstraction; concern response to the general decision situation.

To illustrate these, consider the following narrative:

Red has invaded and occupied two zones of its neighbor, Green. Another neighbor, Yellow, is covertly providing support and shelter to Red leadership. Blue is mounting an air campaign to compel Red to withdraw from Green, to deny it the capability to attack its other neighbors, and to prevent it from transferring C^2 capabilities or materiel to Yellow.

The illustrative biases are the following:

- **Habit bias** (choice). A Bayesian-net model for inferring Red command leadership intent requires the air operations center staff to enter almost a hundred subjective probabilities about Red's response to stimuli. In a previous campaign (against a much different enemy), the (Blue) JFACC had a successful experience with the same model, in which a value of 0.2 had been entered for all the probabilities, so he instructs the model operator to do the same in this case. Habit is an extreme manifestation of bounded rationality—choosing an action because it has been used previously.
- **Regression bias** (adjustment). Development testing suggests that a newly deployed bomb will hit within 5 m of the aimpoint, on average, 85 percent of the time; it is configured to be carried by two different aircraft types, each carrying one bomb, with equal accuracy expected from each. On Day 1, aircraft-type A delivers 100 bombs, with 80 hitting within 5 m; type B delivers 200 bombs, with 180 direct hits. The next day's targets will require an estimated 90 direct hits. Impressed with the bomb's performance when delivered by type B, the JFACC dispatches 100 sorties of the second aircraft type, expecting a 90 percent strike rate. He has ignored the likely regression to the mean—if the aircraft are equally accurate, on average, then the type that

performed better the first day will not do so consistently thereafter.

- **Completeness bias** (confidence). A campaign model provides a prediction of Blue-aircraft Day 1 losses for three candidate MAAPs; it assumes canonical values for Red air-defense capabilities, based on the types and ages of Red's weapons, although the model is capable of higher-resolution estimates with inputs on manpower and weapons maintenance. The model outputs best estimates of 3.04, 3.41, and 2.93 losses, respectively, with 90-percent confidence intervals of ±0.16, 0.22, and 0.16. The JFACC perceives these apparently precise estimates as definitive and curtails the search for more data to inform the decision. An apparently complete set of data inspires undue faith in the quality of the inputs and assumptions that yielded it. Had the display read ~3, ~3½ , and ~3, the JFACC would probably have sought additional input data for higher-resolution calculations.

- **Framing bias** (presentation). A Monte Carlo evaluation of a campaign model compares two MAAPs, each using 100 ground-attack aircraft; for the first plan, the model predicts 95 aircraft surviving Day 1, 85 surviving Day 2, and 70 surviving Day 3; for the second plan, 100 are predicted to survive Day 1; 90, Day 2; and 60, Day 3. The JFACC chooses the first option. Prospect theory suggests that he is risk-averse with respect to gains (survival rates) and risk-seeking with respect to losses; if the outcomes were expressed as losses (fatality rates), he would likely choose the second MAAP.

- **Hindsight bias** (memory). On Day 6, Blue begins to attack fixed ground targets in one occupied zone of Green, in an effort to compel the occupying Red forces to leave, either of their own accord or under orders from higher-level Red leaders. The ATO calls for a total of 24 500-lb precision-guided bombs to be dropped on 18 different targets. After one bomb is dropped on a munitions depot in an abandoned village, the occupying forces retreat in haste from the entire district, leaving behind their artillery. Pleased with the effects achieved with a single well-placed bomb, the JFACC is confident that he had predicted this outcome and that it could hardly have turned out otherwise. He revises the next day's ATO for attacking the other occupied zone, without seeking more information on why the Red forces fled.

- **Base-rate bias** (statistical). On Day 8, the JFACC receives credible intelligence that three men in tan uniforms are in a white Jeep with a black roof, on the highway heading to the border with Yellow. A knowledge-based DSS gives a high likelihood that three wanted Red officials fit the description in the intelligence; the commander dispatches a missile-equipped drone to find and destroy the vehicle and gives firing authority to the drone operator. The JFACC has ignored (or not sought out) the base-rate data—that *most* of the cars in the area match the description in the intelligence.

In these examples, DSSs are explicitly implicated in the habit, completeness, framing, and base-rate biases—the format of the DSS output, the user interface, or the mere fact of employing the DSS stimulates or amplifies the JFACC's propensity to judgmental biases, none of which are clearly benign. More careful design of the DSS could mitigate some of these suboptimal judgments without imposing undue hardships on the JFACC's own decisionmaking style. In the cases of regression and hindsight bias, the JFACC draws possibly biased inferences from valid statistical data and recent observations; in the regression-bias case, a DSS that monitors the data being collected could generate a warning not to misinterpret short-term deviations from average performance. The hindsight-bias case presents a thornier problem, as it is not a matter simply of appropriate data display formats or monitoring calculations: A debiasing DSS would have to force the JFACC to consider alternative explanations for what he observed; various strategies of this sort have been found to at best reduce hindsight bias, and recent studies suggest that they can backfire and *reinforce* biased judgments (Sanna, Schwarz, and Stocker, 2002).

Rethinking Families of Models[1]

Background

The value of having a model family is suggested in Figure B.1. The figure includes not only models and simulations, but also human games and field experiments. In the figure, light is "good" and dark is "bad," so analytical models are depicted as having low resolution, good agility, and breadth for analysis; rather good applicability to decision support; and poor attributes for integration, phenomenology, and human participation. In contrast, field experiments have minimal analytical agility or breadth, are not designed for decision support, and are very good for integration and direct human participation. The point, of course, is that the various tools complement each other.

Analytical organizations are often sizable and can therefore aspire to having an entire suite of appropriate models and war games. Ideally, all the family members would have a known relationship to one another, and some would be cross-calibrated using all available data on the subjects of interest. In fact, some military organizations have had model families for many years, and in some cases they have established relatively routine procedures for calibrating upward. The quality and meaningfulness of the calibrations have varied considerably over time, but the point is that the idea of model families is

---

[1] A preliminary version of this appendix was published as Davis, 2004. The author acknowledges very helpful discussions with colleague Don Stevens.

Figure B.1
Relative Strengths of Illustrative Family Members

Type of model	Reso-lution	Analytical		Decision support	Integra-tion	Phenom-enology	Human action
		Agility	Breadth				
Analytical	Low						
Human game*	Low						
Theater level*	Med.						
Entity level*	High						
Field experiment*	High						

*Simulations

NOTE: assessments depend on many unspecified details. For example, agent-based modeling can raise effectiveness of most models, and small field experiments can be quite agile.

Very bad   Medium   Very good

RAND *MG360-B.1*

hardly new or controversial. For an early example, see Chapter 5 of Hoeber (1981), which describes TAC WARRIOR and the lower-level models that fed it. See also Hughes (1989) and chapters on air, ground, and sea models in Payne (1989). For many years, the German organization IABG maintained an excellent hierarchy of models (Schmitz, Reidelhuber, and Niemeyer, 1984). Currently, the Army's Center for Army Analysis uses detailed models to develop killer-victim scoreboards, which are then used as data structures in RAND's Joint Integrated Contingency Model (JICM) (which has supplanted the venerable CEM). Both RAND and Air Force Studies and Analysis use the BRAWLER model of air-to-air engagements to calibrate more-aggregate-level models, such as Thunder, Storm, START, and JICM. Again, then, the basic idea of model families is not new.

Difficulties in Developing and Maintaining Good Model Families

Although the idea behind model families is old, developing such families has been difficult, for several reasons:

Heterogeneity

Merely collecting models does not a coherent family make. A major problem is heterogeneity in representation, formalism, and substance. Many of the models thrown together as a family have been designed in different paradigms, coded in different languages, and run on computers with different operating systems and input/output facilities. The concepts and names embedded in a given model may have ambiguous relationships to those of other models. Each model and its database depend on numerous assumptions, which may be implicit or poorly documented. Dealing with heterogeneity was discussed as a grand challenge in a recent Dagstuhl workshop (see the report of the Modeling and Simulation Methods Working Group, Fujimoto, Lunceford, Page, and Uhrmacher, 2002).

Management

Although an organization may have viewgraphs extolling the virtues of its model family, the reality may be that different suborganizations are responsible for the various members and may have very little to do with one another. In other organizations, lip service may be given to the desirability of model families, but in practice, virtually all of the available funds go into the organization's core activity, which may be, for example, high-resolution simulation to support experimentation. This may reflect limited budgets and high buy-in costs for high-resolution modeling (e.g., the systems that have evolved from DARPA's early SIMNET work). Concern about such problems was recently expressed in a National Research Council review of naval experimentation (National Research Council, 2004).

Another class of historical management problems is the rejection by analytical organizations of qualitative factors and other manifestations of what the analysts see as nonscientific reasoning. Some of the attitudes have been intellectually based, while others have probably reflected a desire to cloak work in alleged "objectivity" and assure an audit trail to "authoritative algorithms and data," even when there has been no basis for confidence in the results. Often, soft information is actually better than hard data, a fact that becomes important in family-of-models work. Until quite recently, however, U.S. military organizations were extremely unwilling to allow model-based analysis to consider the manifestly low quality of some adversary forces, despite the testimony of history and regional experts.

Sociology

As discussed elsewhere (Davis and Blumenthal, 1991; National Research Council, 1997), the individuals who work on different kinds of models, simulations, games, and experiments typically are members of disputatious tribes. Those skilled at low-resolution exploratory analysis in support of higher-level systems analysis, for example, may be viewed with suspicion by those who work with entity-level simulation and are sensitively aware of the many instances in which details matter. Warfighters may be skilled at war gaming but look askance at models and simulations that omit much of what they believe is crucial or interesting. The ill feelings are reciprocated. Those doing systems analysis may regard those using detailed simulations as hopelessly lost in the weeds and may see war gaming as a merely interesting and nonrigorous activity, often with dysfunctional and illogical doctrine applied mindlessly. Quite aside from unfortunate "feelings," the people who excel at high- and low-level analysis often have very different skill sets and intuitions.

Science and Technology

The underlying military science in a subject area may not be understood, the theory of how to correctly cross-calibrate different models may not be understood, and—even if these are non-problems—the tools for relating and cross-calibrating models may not exist. The result, then, may be little more than observing some high-resolution runs, writing down some outputs, musing a bit, and resetting some inputs to a low-resolution model—more in the manner of getting a rough windspeed measure by holding one's finger up in the air than of anything more respectable. The tools for multiresolution modeling and cross-calibration of models do not currently exist for general, everyday use, although there have been a number of recent research contributions to tools (Haag, Chou, and Preiss, 2002; Treshansky and McGraw, 2002).

Another class of science and technology problems relates to the difficulty associated with representing decisions and behaviors. It remains unclear how best to approach agent-based modeling or how to build tools to make doing so easy. An illustrative issue goes as follows: On the one hand, agents designed top-down with well-controlled, situation-dependent rules or continuous algorithms may be easy to understand, but they have limited potential for learning, adaptation, and "surprising behaviors." On the other hand, agents designed more bottom-up, with simple behavioral rules that lead to different "emergent behaviors" at higher levels, may generate outcomes that are difficult to understand and to investigate rigorously. Which approach is better when? And can a synthesis be achieved? Many other issues can be seen in diverse problem domains (Sanchez and Lucas, 2000).

Despite problems, progress is being made, military applications have been reported (Bullock, McIntyre, and Hill, 2000), and many items from the Marines' Project Albert and other sources can be found online, e.g., at http://www.cna.org/isaac/on-line-papers.htm. Future models and simulations will almost certainly make considerable use of agents.

Tentative Principles for the Next Round

Without elaboration, the following tentative principles may apply for an organization contemplating developing a new model family or substantially updating what it has.

Managing with a Portfolio Approach

As mentioned above, organizations sometimes spend all the available funds on one aspect of modeling and simulation (e.g., entity-level simulation). If model families are to be developed and sustained, however, a portfolio approach is necessary, one in which managers worry about "balance," rather than squeezing the last increment of value out of a particular class within the family. These approaches are contrasted in Figure B.2. In the approach on the left side, all funds go into simulation, and almost all of that into detailed simulation. A better approach is to have a portfolio of activities, as illustrated on the right side. Even a very small group (one to three hot-shot analysts) using small, simple methods might greatly extend the organization's ability to respond to high-level officials and see forests for trees. This effort would benefit from appropriate metamodeling to connect high-resolution work to low-resolution work, which might require a comparable level of effort. A similarly small investment in war gaming might pay big dividends in the quality of work and the connectivity to warfighters. And finally, the balance between maximally complex simulation and smaller simulations that are more focused on problem

Figure B.2
An Illustrative Shift to Having a Portfolio of Models, Simulations, and Modular and Perhaps Composable Systems

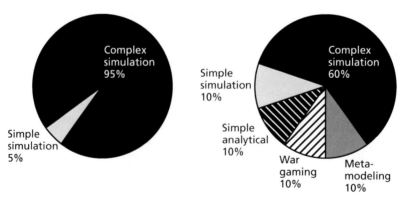

RAND *MG360-B.2*

areas (e.g., countering maneuver with joint fires) would likely be highly desirable. The smaller simulations might be separately developed or, better, the result of using only some modules of more-complex simulations.

How big need the whole be, and how much larger (if any) would funding need to be for the family-of-models approach? The answer, regrettably, would be highly organization dependent.

A given organization, working within its own mission area and a relatively stable relationship to other organizations, should seriously consider investing in new developments that will make its future models modular and perhaps composable. Models designed in an appropriately modular way would facilitate focused and simplified work (e.g., turning off unnecessary complications from other horizontally linked components) and would also facilitate cross-calibration. Such model development, however, will be a major undertaking over a period of years. The issues associated with model composability are discussed critically in a recent study for the Defense Modeling and Simulation Office (Davis and Anderson, 2003).

Multiresolution, Multiperspective Models

If undertaken from the outset with the goal of multiresolution, multiperspective modeling (MRMPM), by which is meant the ability to run models using inputs at different levels of detail, new developments can generate highly flexible models with considerable built-in ability for zoom-in and zoom-out. This cannot be accomplished comprehensively, because of interactions among variables, but a relatively few discrete efforts to build in such MRMPM are both feasible and likely to pay high dividends (Davis and Bigelow, 1998). Significantly, if asked to do so at the outset, designers are in a good position to work out cross-level calibration procedures. They typically understand the issues better than someone who comes along to use the model months or years later. The mechanisms for MRMPM may be simple and even crude—e.g., attaching simple multipliers that allow one to scale related sets of inputs up and down together, thereby reducing the degrees of freedom in exploratory analysis—or they may be much more extensive.

Designing with CAS Concepts

The characteristics of CAS are usually given as (1) sensitivity to initial conditions (and other exogenous events in the course of time); (2) nonlinearity, including discontinuity; (3) "nearly decomposable" hierarchies; (4) agents, meta-agents, and adaptation; (5) aggregation and emergent behaviors; (6) self-organization and phase transitions; and (7) flow, open systems, nonequilibrium, and diversity (Davis, 1997).

Without attempting to summarize the arguments here, let it suffice to note that the following are highly consistent with the lessons learned from CAS theory:

- Because of nonlinearities and sensitivities, models should be designed to support exploratory analysis rather than the search for a classic optimal solution.
- Multiresolution modeling within a given model or simulation, when accompanied by the inclusion of adaptive agents (e.g., decision models representing commanders at different levels), will often be necessary to capture aspects of learning, adaptation, self-organization, and phase transitions. This may be achieved in a single self-contained model or by dynamic compositions.
- Dealing with qualitative and sometimes fuzzy factors is often essential and natural in representing the behavior of agents and the characteristics of uncertain, open, nonequilibrium systems (Davis, 2001).

It is also worth noting a misconception that has served as a red herring in the past: that salvation in modeling and simulation (M&S) consists in detailed bottom-up modeling (millions of entities on the battlefield, all well described). Many of the most celebrated insights from CAS projects to date, in many fields, have come instead as the result of emergent behaviors caused by a small set of elemental behaviors. The entities in question (e.g., automobiles on the highway or armored vehicles on the ground) need not be described in great detail in order to manifest aggregate behaviors of interest (e.g., emergence of swarming tactics by infantry). What is perhaps most interesting here is that resolution is not the point. Yes, it is essential to model at multiple levels of organization and to use agent techniques to insert elemental behaviors, but other details may be irrelevant, depending on the problem.

Designing Around Modern Networking and C⁴ISR

Designing a next generation of M&S around networking and C^4ISR will require as big a shift as the items above. Unfortunately, C^2 has often been assumed perfect or reflected only through some simple static parameters such as delay times for communications, perhaps set differently depending on whether a particular satellite system had been bought. That is not an acceptable representation when asking, for example, about how to measure information dominance or, better, asking how long it will take the United States to do a "Scud hunt" in the next war, as a function of what systems are procured and deployed, how they are operated, and the quality of networking. How to design the new class of models is not a settled question. Figure B.3 (taken from an article by Cebrowski and Garstka (Cebrowski and Garstka, 1998)) illustrates how different a network-centric perspective may be; its implications for modeling and simulation are unclear.

Selected Technical Issues

The remainder of this appendix comments in somewhat more detail on four technical issues of particular importance to the rethinking of model families. These relate to multiresolution, multiperspective modeling; cross-level calibration and the related problem of deterministic versus stochastic modeling at high levels; metamodeling; and making human war gaming serve more-analytical purposes.

Achieving Multiresolution Capabilities

As defined here, multiresolution modeling (MRM), or variable resolution modeling (VRM), allows a user to make inputs at different levels of detail, depending on his needs. Suppose, for example, that one

Figure B.3
One Depiction of the Network-Centric View

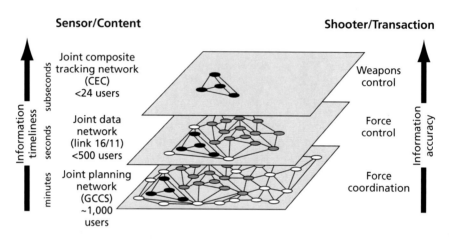

CEC: Cooperative engagement capability
GCCS: Global command and control system

SOURCE: Cebrowski and Garstka, 1998.

RAND MG360-B.3

of the variables of his higher-level depiction is A in Figure B.4. How does the value of that variable get set? At one extreme, A is simply an input parameter. In a multiresolution model, A *may* be input directly, but the user has the option of computing it from more-detailed information. This can be done in several very different ways. Perhaps A is fully determined as a function of B1, B2, and B3, the values of which can be input instead of a single value for A. Or, for some purposes, A may also be considered to be a function of additional factors represented by B4 and B5, which would ordinarily be omitted. These might relate, for example, to logistical issues on the battlefield or to operating with too few ballistic-missile interceptors to launch doctrinal salvos at each incoming attacker. Such considerations would only sometimes be of interest.

Figure B.4 also indicates that B3 might itself be given multi-resolution features: One could enter B3 directly or compute it from C3 and C4. On the lower left, dashes indicate that inputs for B1 and

Figure B.4
Alternative Approaches for Achieving Multiresolution

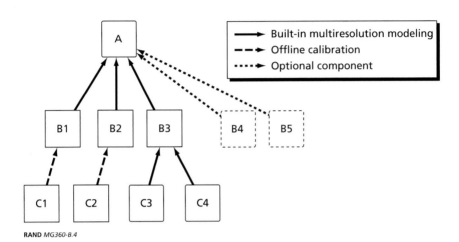

RAND *MG360-B.4*

B2 may be informed by *offline* study of C1 and C2, which may be variables of an entirely different model. We see, then, that multiresolution capability can be achieved by building it into a single model, by modular design, by offline calibration, or by some combination of these methods.

Deterministic Versus Stochastic Representations

A recurring and rather deep issue in multiresolution work is whether higher-level models should be stochastic, or whether it is legitimate for them to be deterministic. This has been discussed frequently over the years, but it is worth rethinking.

Consider first the situation in which one has a high-level (low-resolution) variable A in Figure B.5 (note that the letters and nodes are different from those in Figure B.4), which might be just input directly as a parameter, but which instead is to be calculated by calling a function B that in turn runs a detailed model before setting the value of A in one way or another. That is, the detailed model is run as a subroutine.

Figure B.5 indicates schematically four different ways of proceeding. In Panel 1 (top left), the low-resolution variable A is set at a point in time by calling B (and including, in the call, some information on the situation for which a value is needed). B may look at the information and run the detailed model for a "representative" example. That is, B has numerous high-resolution inputs to specify but

Figure B.5
Alternative Ways to Use High-Resolution Information in a Lower-Resolution Model

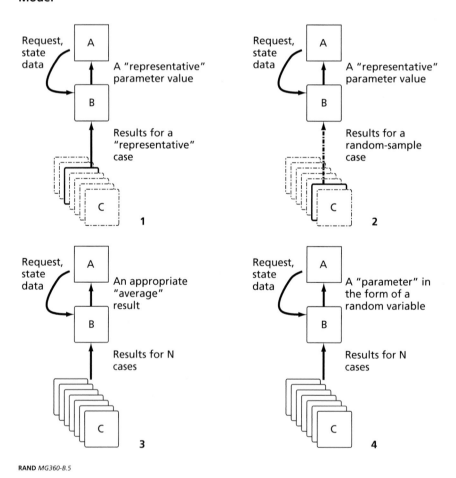

chooses values that seem "representative" for the state in which A is to be evaluated.

In Panel 2, B instead "rolls the dice" to specify the various high-resolution variables, runs the model once with these inputs, and reports back the result, which might or might not be typical. In Panel 3, B runs N different cases, with different dice rolls, and then computes some appropriate value to return to A. This may be a simple average or something more sophisticated that takes into account other aspects of the low-resolution model's state and how the variable A is affecting outputs of interest. In that case, B is serving as a kind of "projection operator." Finally, in Panel 4, B reports back a distribution function for A's value. For example, it might report back, "Use the number 4*R, where R is a normally distributed random variable with mean of 1 and standard deviation of 0.5."

To reiterate, the choices are (1) return a value for A based on a high-resolution run conducted with allegedly representative inputs, (2) return a value for A based on a high-resolution run conducted with randomly chosen inputs, (3) return a value based on N runs and some kind of processing (e.g., averaging), or (4) return a random variable as the value of A.

Obviously, there are major implications for the performance and complexity of the overall model, depending on which approach is taken. Most analysts quickly conclude that they do not want to literally call complex, detailed models as subroutines. An alternative is to run the big model offline many times and generate various data tables. That is, any of the four approaches could be accomplished by running the big model as a subroutine or merely by incorporating data tables based on offline runs. For example, in Panel 2, B would look at a table representing a set of N randomly generated outcomes for the situation in question and would roll the dice to decide which of the outcomes to report.

The problem with this approach is that the tables would represent a preconceived construct of cases. If the simulation is being run with different assumptions or modified algorithms, the low-resolution states may no longer be characterized well by the original cases. Suppose, for example, that a new C^4ISR platform were introduced in the low-resolution model. The presence or non-presence of that super-sensor might not have been anticipated as an issue when the big model was run to develop data tables for various cases. To make this less abstract, consider using a killer-victim scorecard developed for only four cases: meeting engagement and attack on prepared defenses for each of two terrain types, assuming equal information in other respects. If Blue is now given a super-sensor that sees into and through the prepared defenses, the killer-victim scoreboard will be quite wrong. In contrast, it is possible that if the detailed model were invoked as a subroutine, it might have knobs and switches to reflect the new situation. Lookup tables, then, have both strengths and weaknesses.

Having discussed matters in the abstract, let us now look at an example of MRM and alternative approaches. Consider calibrating upward from data generated by detailed models of air war. Assume that we have detailed engagement- and mission-level models. The former determines losses from an engagement *configuration* of, say, N Red and M Blue aircraft, which start the engagement in an *orientation* (e.g., nose-on-nose). Results depend on absolute and relative capabilities of the respective aircraft, including both lethality and survivability factors, avionics, and maneuverability. Ideally, results should also be parameterized by pilot quality and mental status (e.g., aggressive versus timid). The data from the mission-level model determine the distribution of battle configurations and orientations. The mission model's outputs may depend on something like the relative information status, as well as the numbers of Red and Blue aircraft and the sides' intentions and doctrine.

Someone constructing a high-level (low-resolution) model might aspire to tracking daily losses of Red and Blue over time, and doing so with a minimal set of input parameters and values. He might hope to characterize inputs simply with Red and Blue force levels, sortie rates, encounter probabilities per sortie, and relative kill coefficients (or those and survivability coefficients). In that case, the model might be a simple Lanchester-square law or an alternative suggested by colleague Glenn Kent, called the *exponential approximation*.

One version of that has Red's losses ΔR for a particular time period given by

$$\Delta R = (\text{engagements}/\text{unitt ime})G_R(1 - e^{\frac{K_B G_B}{St_B G_R}})\Delta t,$$

where the first factor is the number of engagements per unit time, which depends on force densities, geography, and complicated C^2 issues not discussed here, and where G_R and G_B are the number of Red and Blue in a given engagement, St_B is a "stealth factor" for Blue, and K_B is a kind of kill potential. The quantity

$$G_R(1 - e^{\frac{K_B G_B}{St_B G_R}})$$

is the number of Reds killed by Blue in a given engagement.

The calibration problem, then, would appear to be finding values for K_B, K_R, S_B, and S_R, and if only Blue is assumed to have stealthy aircraft, S_r can be assumed to be 1. The difficulty is that finding values of the remaining three parameters requires averaging outcomes of the detailed models. But how should one calculate those averages? And besides, should not the resulting K_B, K_R, and S_B be stochastic, because of all the hidden variables being averaged over?

The unclassified examples that follow are based not on results of actual high-resolution runs, but on a set of synthetic data (tables such as might have come from a high-resolution model) that were at least superficially plausible: Red and Blue engagement losses for each of four configurations (one Blue to four Red, two Blue to four Red, four Blue to four Red, and one Red to four Blue), each of nine relative orientations (all the combinations of nose, side, and tail, such as nose-tail for an engagement beginning with Blue on Red's tail), and three values of Blue's "stealth parameter," which adjusts the vulnerability of Blue as a function of orientation. Thus, engagement configuration and orientation are treated in some detail, but the stealth factor is treated more crudely. It is not uncommon for data from "high-resolution models" to have such a mixture of detail and crudity, because not all the combinations of potential interest can be run.

A distribution of initial engagement orientations is a function of the relative information status, which was considered to have five different states (Blue dominant, Blue edge, even, Red edge, Red dominant). If the data were real, the distribution would also depend on the detailed capabilities of Red and Blue aircraft for maneuver; detection, tracking, and fire-control; pilot quality and morale; weapon numbers and capabilities; and so on. As is usual (but not right), none of these matters are discussed here. That is, the abstraction issues will assume that these matters are constant and reflected in the data.

The results of the experiment—which, in the interest of keeping this appendix to a reasonable length, are not discussed in depth here—illustrate generic problems and principles:

- **What "truth" are the results calibrated from?** The biggest error in attempting to calibrate upward may be to assume that the high-resolution models are "correct." In practice, they often do not deal correctly, if at all, with key issues (e.g., pilot quality and aggressiveness or the frequency of engagements as a function of strategy and geography). When this is the case, the upward calibration may not be realistic, and the "calibrated" coefficients should still be treated as uncertain parameters, albeit with a "peg point" to nominal detail.

- **Not all aggregations are equal.** The next biggest error in abstraction may be that of adopting "naïve aggregations," such as the one described above (assuming Lanchester equations at the top level), which makes no explicit mention of the relative balance of information or the configurations of battle. These factors matter so much and are so uncertain that they deserve to appear even in aggregate-level models. Aggregate should not mean dumb.

- **Proper aggregations may require anticipation of context.** It is superficially appealing to do aggregations on standalone forces, but the worth of a weapon system or unit depends on the context in which it finds itself. Suppose that at the aggregate level, one reasoned that Red's information superiority would mean that one-half of the engagement orientations would be against

Blue's tail and the other half would be "even" cases, such as nose-on-nose, as distinct from Blue-nose-on-Red-tail. That would underestimate the value of Red's information, because in the real world, Red would try never to engage Blue except from the tail or side. Volitional nose-on-nose engagements would be suicide against a stealthy Blue. The moral here is that upward calibration requires various mappings that require understanding of context. Analogous problems in characterizing ground forces with static measures led in earlier years to "situational force scoring" (Allen, 1995).

- **Point values should reflect underlying distributions.** If, nonetheless, point values are used for the kill coefficients, then it is a serious error to use the allegedly most likely or allegedly typical configuration and orientation unless there is reason to believe that these matters can be tightly controlled. The coefficient values for these cases are often peak values of distributions with long tails. Thus, point values, if used, should be something like means or medians of the underlying distributions.

- **Aggregate-level stochastic calculations are not usually worthwhile** (given the caveat of the preceding item). There is usually little analytical benefit to making the aggregate-level kill coefficients stochastic (Hughes, 1994). Rather, it is more straightforward and insightful to show results parameterizing the kill coefficients and to label the curves so as to indicate circumstances to which they apply (e.g., Blue information dominance versus equal Red and Blue information). In the illustrative problem, this could happen if the aggregate model still keeps track of information status, the correct value of which is highly uncertain.

But sometimes stochastic analysis is important. Stochastic aggregate-level calculations are sometimes valuable—for example, in dramatizing a bifurcation of outcomes that is smoothed over by expected-value calculations. Using the Lanchester-square aggregate model of air war, if the aggregate-level coefficients suggest an exchange ratio of 3, then if the ratio of Red and Blue aircraft is 3:1, the model will predict a mutual drawdown. A stochastic treatment would predict a bimodal outcome in which either Red or Blue wins quickly and decisively, with equal likelihood. The moral here is that one should not depend on expected-value calculations, even for qualitative insight, near those alleged breakeven points. There are many other instances as well in which stochastic calculations are important (Horrigan, 1991; Lucas, 2000).

Most of these points can be seen in Figure B.6, which shows the force ratio (Red to Blue) on Day 2 as calculated in a number of different ways, assuming an initial force ratio of 4:1 and the synthetic data mentioned above. The leftmost set of bars is the "exact" calculation. The next set is based on a "smart" aggregate model that includes information status as an explicit variable. Moving rightward, the next set is based on a standard (naïve) aggregate model in which the kill coefficients have been given nominal point values based on detailed engagement-level results for allegedly typical cases (in this case, nose-on-nose engagements). The next set of bars is a variant in which the point values were chosen as the means or averages over a distribution of engagements (assumed here to be Blue superior, even, and Red superior in the proportions 0.5, 0.26, and 0.24). Finally, the rightmost set of bars shows the mean of a stochastic calculation that does not depend explicitly on information status but has random fluctuations reflecting that hidden variable. The very last bar on the right is different from the others; it merely shows the size of the standard deviation for the stochastic calculations.

All but the first set of bars come from aggregate models, but results vary greatly. Moreover, it is obvious from the sensitivities that information status should be an aggregate-level variable. Anything that smoothes over it is at best a naïve aggregation and possibly a very bad one. By comparing the two sets of bars based on "point calculations," one sees how assuming a "nominal" case that is actually a very favorable case can bias results substantially. Setting the kill coefficient to be the mean value of the underlying distribution does a better job if, in fact, there is a distribution of information statuses and one can estimate it. The mean of the stochastic calculation is even larger

Figure B.6
Comparing "Exact" and Approximate Estimates of Exchange Ratio

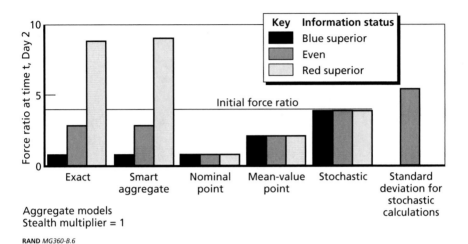

RAND *MG360-B.6*

because that calculation includes cases in which Red wins decisively (very high force ratio, even by Day 2, as indicated by the first two sets of bars for the case of Red superior). Note that the standard deviation of the stochastic calculation is huge. This is because there is a bifurcation: Either Blue wins decisively (very small force ratio) or Red wins decisively (large force ratio). This insight, however, is probably better seen from the "smart aggregation" that maintains dependence on information status. Bothering with the stochastic calculation is not obviously useful. In contrast, the stochastic calculation is a great deal more informative than the probably more usual point calculations.

Metamodeling, Motivated and Otherwise
The previous section discussed calibrating upward from a detailed model to a lower-resolution model. An overlapping but philosophically separate track has been that of building statistical metamodels. One runs the detailed model, collects data, and finds a statistical model that represents reasonably the detailed-model results, preferably with many fewer parameters to be varied. The result is called a statistical metamodel, response surface, or repro model, depending on

one's community. Building such statistical metamodels often seems attractive, because it does not require deep thinking or theorizing about the substantive problem: It can be an exercise in applying statistical tools to some "data." In some cases, the results are quite useful, and in some cases the approach can yield insights about what variables are and are not important or what composite variables should be seen as important. The approach, however, has some serious drawbacks for analysts and the decisionmakers they serve. In particular, the statistical metamodels may not be understandable. They may give predictions but few insights or explanations. They may also be erroneous in subtle "corners" of the problem space that happen to be of particular importance. It is much preferable, in our view, to develop "motivated metamodels" that build in a reasonable structure for the metamodel, based on "physical reasoning" and concern for problem context, such as the possibility of nonlinear effects arising from the existence of critical components in a system, each of which must perform adequately to avoid system failure. If one begins with such a tentative structure and then applies the same statistical techniques, the result can be a very good metamodel that also conveys a story. This approach is discussed in detail in Davis and Bigelow (2003). Other approaches to statistical metamodeling are also being studied (Fall and Plotz, 2001; Haag, Chou, and Preiss, 2002; Trevisani, Sisti, and Mayhew, 2002).

Analytic War Gaming

The last special topic to be discussed here is how to make human war gaming more "analytic." This deserves an entire paper, but the key ideas suggested here, which relate to Figure B.7, can be summarized as follows:

- Design the games as vignettes, with relatively well-described situations.
- Use competing teams (e.g., U.S., UK, Israel, Poland) to see diverse tactics and assumptions.
- Encourage the teams to explicitly develop contingent plans (e.g., with branches and sequels).

Figure B.7
A Process for Using Human War Gaming Analytically

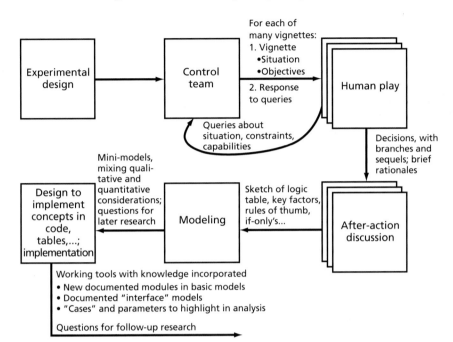

RAND MG360-B.7

- Protect the teams organizationally, perhaps by embedding them in independent groups such as FFRDCs or even war colleges, or the U.S. Joint Forces Command (JFCOM).
- Record planning factors and reasoning used during team play, recognizing them as the germs of "models" that can later be formalized, whether quantitatively or qualitatively (Davis, 2001, 2002b, 2003). Accept overarching "soft" factors.
- Use Red teams, both to better appreciate different ways of assessing the situation and defining objectives and to draw upon expertise about adversary military doctrine. Red teams apply well to counterterrorism as well, as is being demonstrated in a study led by James Miller (Murray, 2002; Sinnreich, 2002; Murdock, 2003).
- Follow up with analysis and modeling.

Analysis should come at the beginning and the end (Figure B.7). People skilled in capabilities analysis should design the war games and vignettes to cover the space adequately (perhaps with a combination of experimental design and M&S greatly narrowing the number of cases). Analytically inclined people with an appreciation of, and openness toward, soft factors should record intragame logic and then develop summary qualitative models. Subsequently, modelers should explicitly relate the variables of the human games to variables of models and simulations—adding variables to the latter as necessary, e.g., using "interface models." Much more can be done in these respects than is commonly appreciated, at least with some models. For example, in the form of colleague Carl Jones' "J-language," JICM includes numerous "hooks" for qualitative factors and allows for contingent strategies that can be specified by the analysts rather than using hardwired databases developed months earlier.

Conclusions

Much more can and should be written about how to develop families of models and games, but this monograph has at least identified ideas that may be useful to an organization contemplating doing so. They include (1) taking a portfolio approach that encourages maintaining a balance among low-resolution agile models, detailed simulation, war gaming, and the like; (2) designing with exploratory analysis and zoom capabilities in mind from the outset; and (3) assuring that C^4ISR, networking, and adaptive behaviors (e.g., as obtained with "agents") are central concepts of architectures. At the next level of detail, our admonitions include suggestions for multiresolution modeling, for both deterministic and stochastic analysis; the use of metamodels, particularly motivated metamodels; and using human war gaming analytically to shape and inform subsequent qualitative and quantitative models and smarter agents.

All of this has many implications for M&S technology, which is needed, for example, to help in aggregation, disaggregation, meta-modeling, explanation, composition, and data mining from war games.

Further Discussion of Judgmental Bias and DSS

The main text discusses biases and the potential for reducing the bias of decisionmaker judgments through the use of DSS. Much more could be said, however, and we note a few points here.

Reasons for the Superiority of Frequentist Depictions

Neuroscience suggests that people have a collection of mental modules for various cognitive functions, including reasoning, that perform better with information in formats that ancestral humans adapted to. Humans have had considerable direct experience with "natural" frequencies ("the river flooded four years out of the last 20"), whereas probabilities are considerably more abstract ("the probability of the river flooding in any year is 0.2") (Gigerenzer, 1994). The frequency formulation, in this case at least, contains more contextualizing information, in both the numerator and the denominator, and fits better with cognition. As noted in the text, however, this perspective is disputed.

The Subset Bias, Conjunction Bias, and Sensemaking

With the "conjunction fallacy," people estimate the likelihood of an object having two independent properties as higher than that of its having at least one of them. A common illustration is the "Linda problem," in which several of Linda's attributes are given, and subjects are asked to rank-order statements about Linda according to their probability. Most subjects rank "feminist and bank teller" higher than "bank teller," even when it is made clear that choosing "bank teller" does not rule out "feminist also" (Tversky and Kahneman, 1983). Once again, the frequentist formulation greatly mitigates the bias. If the question is, "100 people fit the description above; how many are bank tellers, how many are feminist bank tellers?" the subset bias observed is much weaker (Fiedler, 1988).

Explanations for the subset bias vary. Specific scenarios may seem more likely than general ones because they better represent the way we imagine events (Tversky and Kahneman, 1983). Certainly, war games are more salient and powerful when they include colorful details, even though that reduces the likelihood of the scenario used being "correct."

The conjunctive label (bank teller *and* feminist) may also provide a more compelling pattern match to a real person, triggering the pattern-match heuristic and thereby leading to an overestimate of probability (Lopes and Oden, 1991). However, with a frequentist depiction of issues, subjects may be thinking about a large sample and may be less likely to employ a pattern-matching heuristic in the first place.

Another argument is that even if people recognize that the conjunction is slightly less probable, they sense that it has greater "expected informativeness" (Bar-Hillel and Neter, 1993). We see here the connection to storytelling, which achieves greater effectiveness in making points by adding color and narrative. If the point made is not really dependent upon the color and narrative but is valid, then the enrichment is all to the good. But if one's pattern of thought is to look for stories, then it is perhaps not surprising if one is guilty of the conjunction fallacy.

Although the military decisionmaking literature does not address the subset bias explicitly, the possible relevance to operational decisionmaking is clear. For example, a commander receiving battle-damage assessments may infer from the fact that bombs fell where targeted and the adversary has not maneuvered in the last 12 hours that he has successfully decapitated the enemy and broken his C^2 system. The reality may be that the adversary commander was not in the targets struck, that the C^2 system was merely inconvenienced, and that a new ground-force maneuver is being planned for execution tomorrow morning. In this case, then, the commander is motivated to infer more than the data suggest and, in doing so, to construct a more compelling story that fits his intentions, perhaps at the expense of correctness.

The Columbia Disaster and Its Lessons

A prominent recent event highlights the potentially severe consequences of judgmental biases, with special relevance to military operations. In testimony before the independent panel on the breakup of the space shuttle Columbia, an expert advisor to NASA said that NASA had

> again fallen prey to "systemic" flaws in reasoning—such as the creeping acceptance of poorly understood risks in operating the space shuttle . . . despite prodigious efforts and the best of intentions, [NASA] had failed to upgrade its aged database and computer systems to allow it to track subtle but unacceptable trends . . . the shuttle team has been lulled by repeated successes. "I think there's a flaw in the reasoning of many well-intentioned people" in forgetting that "if you've a 1 in 100 chance of risk of an event occurring, the event can occur on the first or the last [opportunity], and there's an equal probability each time.". . . the perception within the agency seemed to be "that if I've flown 20 times, the risk is less than if I've just flown once. And we were continually attempting to inform them that unless they've changed the risk positively, they still have the same issue even after 50 flights or 60 flights" (Sawyer, 2003).

Several judgmental biases might have been at play here, most notably the overconfidence bias and the disjunction bias, which holds that probability is often underestimated in compound disjunctive problems (Tversky and Kahneman, 1974). NASA engineers and military commanders are equally highly trained, disciplined, and responsible, and yet both are subject to a biasing organizational dynamic—the pressure to weight observed successes more heavily than is warranted. Imagine a commander deploying an innovative new platform in combat for the first time. Development testing suggests that it should fail in about 5 to 10 percent of its sorties against enemy surface-to-air missiles. It survives its first three combat sorties; should this success embolden the commander to rely on it more than he had been inclined to before the first flight? Certainly not—but his inclination to do so should not be surprising. It is no challenge for a DSS to make the apposite calculations, but to convey the results in a compelling manner is nontrivial.

More generally (i.e., not limited to military applications), while many DSSs are intended to mitigate the effects of judgmental biases, there has been little consideration of how their use may contribute to biased decisionmaking (a promising study of biases in the judgment of medical patients by practitioners using DSSs is under way (Ubel, 2002)). A consideration of judgmental biases is not evident in many discussions of military operational DSSs, even for those that account for a variety of users' idiosyncrasies. For instance, the Attack Operations Decision Aid (AODA) (Cho, 1999) is a tool to assist in diverting air assets from missions already specified in an ATO to time-critical targets (Hura, McLeod, Mesic, Sauer, Jacobs, Norton, and Hamilton, 2002). While the tool is forward-deployed on airborne platforms and used for routine targeting decisions, very high-value, high-risk, or politically sensitive targets bring the JFACC or higher-level commanders into the decision process. The tool both supplements and supplants the commander's own decisionmaking capabilities:

> AODA's algorithms are based on operations research techniques. A commander makes similar decisions using a heuristic approach which, while adequate in a non-stressing (few-on-few) environment, can not efficiently handle complex situations. AODA assesses the tradeoffs among original target value and new target value, available weapon capability, asset survivability, and probability of destruction. AODA then provides the operator with a list of recommended weapon target pairings.

AODA's algorithms require that the values of targets and assets be captured numerically. Although subjective valuations of this nature are made by commanders during the decision process, they are not quantified to the level required by the decision aid. To fully support the aid's algorithms, commanders will have to explicitly state the values they place on targets and assets (Pedersen, Van Zandt, Vogel, and Williamson, 1999).

These sorts of subjective valuations (even by experts) are prone to a broad range of judgmental biases. It is not evident whether these potential biases are explicitly considered in the tool's design, although they should certainly figure in many of the other individual-level factors that influence its effectiveness.

The decision aid must meet the user's perceived needs and incorporate those factors that the user feels are critical to a correct decision. It is imperative to determine what the user thinks the decision-support needs are, the conditions under which the aid is needed, the features that are needed, and the factors that the aid's algorithms should consider. A decision aid should be built with a clear understanding of the users' expectations and level of expertise, as well as the operating environment.

Decision aids may support various levels of command. At low levels, decision aids may simply help the operators to recognize a critical situation, so that preplanned appropriate action can be taken and important information can be elevated to other command levels. Decision aids that support a commander responsible for the execution of the campaign plan may need to gather all the available data, organize and present information clearly, and recommend options that facilitate decisionmaking. A decision aid's level of sophistication needs to be geared to the user's training, educational level, and background, which vary with the command level (Pedersen, Van Zandt, Vogel, and Williamson, 1999).

With regard to the latter point, higher levels of command historically have favored analytical decisionmaking over naturalistic decisionmaking, which should also influence the nature and sophistication of the appropriate DSS, but ongoing advances in information technology are blurring the distinctions among the levels and are causing them to merge (MacGregor, 1992).

Bibliography

Alberts, David S., John J. Garstka, Richard E. Hayes, and David A. Signori, *Understanding Information Age Warfare*, Washington, DC: Department of Defense, CCRP Publication Series, 2001.

Alberts, David S., John J. Garstka, and Frederick Stein, *Network Centric Warfare: Developing and Leveraging Information Technology*, Washington, DC: Department of Defense, CCRP Publication Series, 1999.

Alberts, David S., and Richard E. Hayes, *Power to the Edge: Command and Control in the Information Age*, Washington, DC: Department of Defense, Command and Control Research Program, 2003.

Alexander, Steven M., and David O. Ross, "Modeling Soft Factors in Computer Based Wargames," in Alex F. Sisti and Dawn A. Trevisani, eds., *Proceedings of SPIE*, Vol. 4716: *Enabling Technologies for Simulation Science VI*, 2002, pp. 94–98.

Allen, Patrick, "The Need to Represent a Wide Range of Battle Types in Air-Ground Combat Models," *Military Operations Research Journal*, Vol. 1, No. 3, 1995.

Allison, Graham, and Philip D. Zelikow, *Essence of Decision: Explaining the Cuban Missile Crisis*, 2d ed. (1st ed., 1971), Reading, MA: Addison Wesley, Longman, 1999.

Arkes, Hal R., Robyn M. Dawes, and Caryn Christensen, "Factors Influencing the Use of a Decision Rule in a Probabilistic Task," *Organizational Behavior and Human Decision Processes*, Vol. 37, No. 1, 1986, pp. 93–110.

Arnott, David, "Decision Biases and Decision Support Systems Development," Melbourne, Australia: Monash University, Decision Support Systems Laboratory, Working Paper, 2002.

Arnott, David, *A Taxonomy of Decision Biases*, Technical report, Melbourne, Australia: Monash University, School of Information Management and Systems, 1998.

Arthur, W. Brian, "Complexity and the Economy," *Science*, Vol. 284, 1999, pp. 107–109.

Bankes, Stephen C., "Exploratory Modeling for Policy Analysis," *Operations Research*, Vol. 41, No. 3, 1993, pp. 435–449.

Bar-Hillel, Maya, and Efrat Neter, "How Alike It Is Versus How Likely It Is: A Disjunction Fallacy in Probability Judgments," *Journal of Personality and Social Psychology*, Vol. 65, No. 6, 1993, pp. 1119–1131.

Barsnick, Amy, *Modeling Human Elements in Decision-Making*, Monterey, Calif.: Naval Postgraduate School, Masters Thesis, 2002.

Bar-Yam, Yaneer, *Dynamics of Complex Systems* (Studies in Nonlinearity), Boulder, CO: Westview Press, 1997.

Bigelow, James H., and Paul K. Davis, *Implications for Model Validation of Multiresolution, Multiperspective Modeling (MRMPM) and Exploratory Analysis*, Santa Monica, Calif.: RAND Corporation, MR-1570-AF, 2003.

Birkler, John L., C. Richard Neu, and Glenn A. Kent, *Gaining New Military Capability: An Experiment in Concept Development*, Santa Monica, Calif.: RAND Corporation, MR-912-OSD, 1998.

Bisantz, Ann M., James Llinas, Younho Seong, Richard Finger, and Jiun-Jian Jian, *Empirical Investigations of Trust-Related System Vulnerabilities in Aided, Adversarial Decision Making*, Buffalo, NY: State University of New York, 2000.

Bormann, Ernest G., *Discussion and Group Methods: Theory and Practice*, New York: Harper & Row, 1969.

Brandenberger, Adam M., and Barry J. Nalebuff, "The Right Game: Use Game Theory to Shape Strategy," *Harvard Business Review*, July–August, 1995, pp. 57–71.

Brase, Gary L., "Which Statistical Formats Facilitate What Decisions? The Perception and Influence of Different Statistical Information Formats,"

Journal of Behavioral Decision Making, Vol. 15, No. 5, 2002, pp. 381–401.

Bullock, Richard K., Gregory McIntyre, and Raymond R. Hill, "Using Agent-Based Modeling to Capture Airpower Strategic Effects," *Proceedings of Winter Simulation Conference*, J. A. Joines, R. R. Barton, K. Kang, and P. Fishwick, eds., 2000, pp. 1739–1746.

Camerer, Colin F., "Individual Decision Making," in John H. Kagel and Alvin E. Roth, eds., *Handbook of Experimental Economics*, Princeton, NJ: Princeton University Press, 1995, pp. 587–703.

Cassandros, Christos, *Stochastic Fidelity Preservation in Mixed Resolution Simulation Modeling*, Burlington, MA: Network Dynamics, Final Report on SBIR Contract F30602-99-C0097, 2000.

Casscells, W., A. Schoenberger, and T. Grayboys, "Interpretation by Physicians of Clinical Laboratory Results," *New England Journal of Medicine*, Vol. 299, 1978, pp. 999–1000.

Cebrowski, Arthur K., and John Garstka, "Network-Centric Warfare: Its Origins and Future," *Naval Institute Proceedings*, Annapolis, MD: U.S. Naval Institute, 1998, pp. 28–35.

Cho, Chien-Ching, "Choose Your Weapons and Targets," *The Edge*, Vol. 3, No. 2, 1999, p. 12.

Cohen, Marvin S., "A Situation Specific Model of Trust in Decision Aids," *Proceedings of the International Conference on Human Performance, Situation Awareness and Automation*, Vancouver, British Columbia, Canada, 2002.

Cohen, Marvin S., *Training Critical Thinking for the Battlefield*, Vol. I: *Basis in Cognitive Theory and Research*, Arlington, VA: Cognitive Technologies, 2000.

Cohen, Marvin S., "The Bottom Line: Naturalistic Decision Aiding," in Gary Klein, Judith Orasanu, Roberta Calderwood, and Caroline E. Zsambok, eds., *Decision Making in Action: Models and Methods*, Norwood, NJ: Ablex Publishing, 1993, pp. 265–269.

Cohen, William, *Report of the Quadrennial Defense Review*, Washington, DC: Department of Defense, 1997.

Cosmides, Leda, and John Tooby, "Are Humans Good Intuitive Statisticians After All? Rethinking Some Conclusions from the Literature on

Judgment Under Uncertainty," *Cognition*, Vol. 58, No. 1, 1996, pp. 1–73.

Dacey, Raymond, and Lisa J. Carlson, "Traditional Decision Analysis and the Poliheuristic Theory of Foreign Policy Decision Making," *Journal of Conflict Resolution*, Vol. 48, No. 1, 2004, pp. 38–55.

Davis, Paul K., "Rethinking Families of Models," in Dawn A. Trevisani and Alex F. Sisti, eds., *Proceedings of SPIE*, Vol. 5423: *Enabling Technologies for Simulation Science VIII*, 2004, pp. 17–31.

Davis, Paul K., "Exploratory Analysis and Implications for Modeling," in Stuart Johnson, Martin Libicki, and Gregory Treverton, eds., *New Challenges, New Tools for Defense Decisionmaking*, Santa Monica, Calif.: RAND Corporation, 2003a, pp. 255–283.

Davis, Paul K., "Thoughts on Higher-Level Adversary Modeling," in Alex F. Sisti and Dawn A. Trevisani, eds., *Proceedings of SPIE*, Vol. 5091: *Enabling Technologies for Simulation Science VII*, 2003b, pp. 172–181.

Davis, Paul K., "Uncertainty-Sensitive Planning," in Stuart Johnson, Martin Libicki, and Gregory Treverton, eds., *New Challenges, New Tools for Defense Decisionmaking*, Santa Monica, Calif.: RAND Corporation, 2003c, pp. 131–155.

Davis, Paul K., *Analytic Architecture for Capabilities-Based Planning, Mission-System Analysis, and Transformation*, Santa Monica, Calif.: RAND Corporation, 2002a.

Davis, Paul K., "Synthetic Cognitive Modeling of Adversaries for Effects-Based Planning," in Alex F. Sisti and Dawn A. Trevisani, eds., *Proceedings of SPIE*, Vol. 4716: *Enabling Technologies for Simulation Science VI*, 2002b.

Davis, Paul K., *Effects-Based Operations: A Grand Challenge for the Analytical Community*, Santa Monica, Calif.: RAND Corporation, 2001.

Davis, Paul K., "Implications of Complex-Adaptive System Research for Defense Analysis," Briefing to the MORS Warfare Analysis and Complexity Mini-Symposium, Military Operations Research Society, 1997.

Davis, Paul K., *Aggregation, Disaggregation, and the 3:1 Rule in Ground Combat*, Santa Monica, Calif.: RAND Corporation, MR-638-AF/A/OSD, 1995.

Davis, Paul K., "Planning for Adaptiveness," in Paul K. Davis (ed.), *New Challenges for Defense Planning: Rethinking How Much Is Enough*, Santa Monica, Calif.: RAND Corporation, 1994a.

Davis, Paul K., "Protecting the Great Transition," in Paul K. Davis (ed.), *New Challenges for Defense Planning: Rethinking How Much Is Enough*, Santa Monica, Calif.: RAND Corporation, 1994b.

Davis, Paul K., *Studying First-Strike Stability with Knowledge-Based Models of Human Decisionmaking*, Santa Monica, Calif.: RAND Corporation, 1989.

Davis, Paul K., and Robert H. Anderson, *Improving the Composability of Department of Defense Models and Simulations*, Santa Monica, Calif.: RAND Corporation, 2003.

Davis, Paul K., and James H. Bigelow, *Motivated Metamodels: Synthesis of Cause-Effect Reasoning and Statistical Metamodeling*, Santa Monica, Calif.: RAND Corporation, MR-1570-AF, 2003.

Davis, Paul K., and James H. Bigelow, *Experiments in Multiresolution Modeling (MRM)*, Santa Monica, Calif.: RAND Corporation, MR-1004-DARPA, 1998.

Davis, Paul K., James H. Bigelow, and Jimmie McEver, *Exploratory Analysis and a Case History of Multiresolution, Multiperspective Modeling*, Santa Monica, Calif.: RAND Corporation, RP-925, 2001.

Davis, Paul K., and Donald Blumenthal, *The Base of Sand: A White Paper on the State of Military Combat Modeling*, Santa Monica, Calif.: RAND Corporation, N-3148-OSD/DARPA, 1991.

Davis, Paul K., and Lou Finch, *Defense Planning for the Post-Cold War Era: Giving Meaning to Flexibility, Adaptiveness, and Robustness of Capability*, Santa Monica, Calif.: RAND Corporation, 1993.

Davis, Paul K., David Gompert, and Richard Kugler, *Adaptiveness in National Defense: The Basis of a New Framework*, Santa Monica, Calif.: RAND Corporation, IP-155, 1996.

Davis, Paul K., and Zalmay Khalilzad, *A Composite Approach to Air Force Mid- and Long-Term Planning*, Santa Monica, Calif.: RAND Corporation, MR-787-AF, 1996.

Davis, Paul K., Richard Kugler, and Richard Hillestad, *Issues and Options for the Quadrennial Defense Review*, Santa Monica, Calif.: RAND Corporation, DB-201-OSD, 1997.

Davis, Paul K., Jimmie McEver, and Barry Wilson, *Measuring Interdiction Capabilities in the Presence of Anti-Access Strategies: Exploratory Analysis to Inform Adaptive Strategies for the Persian Gulf*, Santa Monica, Calif.: RAND Corporation, 2002.

Davis, Paul K., and James A. Winnefeld, *The RAND Strategy Assessment Center: An Overview and Interim Conclusions About Utility and Development Options*, Santa Monica, Calif.: RAND Corporation, R-2945-DNA, 1983.

Defense Science Board, *Discriminate Use of Force*, Washington, DC: Office of the Under Secretary of Defense for Acquisition and Technology, 2003.

Deptula, David, "Effects-Based Operations: Change in the Nature of Warfare," *Aerospace Education Foundation*, online at http://www.afa.org/media/reports/, as of 2001.

Dewar, James A., *Assumption-Based Planning: A Tool for Reducing Avoidable Surprises*, Cambridge, UK: Cambridge University Press, 2002.

Dixit, Avinash K., and Barry J. Nalebuff, *Thinking Strategically: The Competitive Edge in Business, Politics, and Everyday Life*, New York: W.W. Norton, 1991.

Dixon, Norman, *On the Psychology of Military Incompetence*, New York: Basic Books, 1976.

Dreyer, Paul, and Paul K. Davis, *A Portfolio-Analysis Tool for Missile Defense (PAT-MD): Methodology and User's Manual*, Santa Monica, Calif.: RAND Corporation, TR-262-MDA, forthcoming.

Dubik, James, "Effects-Based Decisions and Actions," *Military Review*, January–February, 2003, pp. 33–36.

Dzindolet, Mary T., Scott A. Peterson, Regina A. Pomranky, Linda G. Pierce, and Hall P. Beck, "The Role of Trust in Automation Reliance," *International Journal of Human-Computer Studies*, Vol. 58, No. 6, 2003, pp. 697–718.

Eisenhardt, Kathleen M., and Mark J. Zbaracki, "Strategic Decision Making," *Strategic Management Journal*, Vol. 13, 1992, pp. 17–37.

Enthoven, Alain, and K. Wayne Smith, *How Much Is Enough: Shaping the Defense Program*, 1961–1969, New York: Harper and Row, 1971.

Evans, Jonathan St. B.T., Simon J. Handley, Nick Perham, David E. Over, and Valerie A. Thompson, "Frequency Versus Probability Formats in Statistical Word Problems," *Cognition*, Vol. 77, No. 3, 2000, pp. 197–213.

Fagin, Ronald, Joseph Y. Halpern, and Nimrod Megiddo, "A Logic for Reasoning About Probabilities," *Information Systems Research*, Vol. 87, Nos. 1–2, 1990, pp. 78–128.

Fall, Tom, and Gary A. Plotz, "A Multi-Level Resolution Demonstration of the Utility of C4ISR," in Alex F. Sisti and Dawn A. Trevisani, eds., *Proceedings of SPIE*, Vol. 4367: *Enabling Technologies for Simulation Science V*, 2001, pp. 104–112.

Fiedler, Klaus, "The Dependence of the Conjunction Fallacy on Subtle Linguistic Factors," *Psychological Research*, Vol. 50, 1988, pp. 123–129.

Fischhoff, Baruch, "Heuristics and Biases in Application," in Thomas Gilovich, Dale Griffin, and Daniel Kahneman, eds., *Heuristics and Biases: The Psychology of Intuitive Judgment*, New York: Cambridge University Press, 2002, pp. 730–748.

Fischhoff, Baruch, "Prejudices About Bias," College Park, MD: University of Maryland, Institute for Philosophy & Public Policy, Working Paper, 1997.

Fisher, Craig W., InduShobha Chengalur-Smith, and Donald P. Ballou, "The Impact of Experience and Time on the Use of Data Quality Information in Decision Making," *Information Systems Research*, Vol. 14, No. 2, 2003, pp. 170–188.

Fisher, Gene Harvey, *Cost Considerations in Systems Analysis*, New York: Elsevier, 1971.

Forrester, Jay Wright, *Urban Dynamics*, Cambridge, MA: Wright Allen Press, 1969.

Friel, John, "Air Battle Models," in Wayne Hughes (ed.), *Military Modeling*, 2d ed., Alexandria, VA: Military Operations Research Society, 1989, pp. 113–128.

Frostic, Fred, Kevin Lewis, and Christopher J. Bowie, *The New Calculus: Analyzing Airpower's Changing Role in Joint Theater Campaigns*, Santa Monica, Calif.: RAND Corporation, 1993.

Fujimoto, Richard M., Dell Lunceford, Ernest H. Page, and Adelinde Uhrmacher, "Grand Challenges for Modeling and Simulation," Schloss Dagstuhl International Conference and Research Center for Computer Science, online at http://www.informatik.uni-rostock.de/~lin/GC/report/index.html, as of 2002.

Gershon, Nahum, and Stephen G. Eick, "Visualization's New Tack: Making Sense of Information," *IEEE Spectrum*, Vol. 32, No. 11, 1995, pp. 38–56.

Gigerenzer, Gerd, "Surrogates for Theories," *Theory & Psychology*, Vol. 8, No. 2, 1998, pp. 195–204.

Gigerenzer, Gerd, "On Narrow Norms and Vague Heuristics: A Rebuttal to Kahneman and Tversky," *Psychological Review*, Vol. 103, No. 3, 1996, pp. 592–596.

Gigerenzer, Gerd, "Why the Distinction Between Single-Event Probabilities and Frequencies Is Important for Psychology (and Vice Versa)," in George Wright and Peter Ayton, eds., *Subjective Probability*, New York: John Wiley & Sons, 1994, pp. 129–161.

Gigerenzer, Gerd, and Reinhard Selten, *Bounded Rationality: The Adaptive Toolbox*, Cambridge, MA: MIT Press, 2002.

Gigerenzer, Gerd, Peter M. Todd, and ABC Research Group, *Simple Heuristics That Make Us Smart*, Oxford, UK: Oxford University Press, 1999.

Goeller, Bruce F., et al., *Policy Analysis of Water Management for the Netherlands, Summary Report*, Santa Monica, Calif.: RAND Corporation, R-2500/1-NETH, 1983.

Gordon, John, and Brian Nichiporuk, *Alternative Futures and Their Implications for Army Modernization*, Santa Monica, Calif.: RAND Corporation, 2003.

Gorry, G. Anthony, and Michael S. Scott-Morton, "A Framework for Management Information Systems," *Sloan Management Review*, Vol. 13, No. 1, 1971, pp. 55–70.

Gouran, Dennis S., "Reflections on the Type of Question as a Determinant of the Form of Interaction in Decision-Making and Problem-Solving

Discussions," *Communication Quarterly*, Vol. 51, No. 2, 2003, pp. 111–125.

Graesser, Arthur, Brent Olde, and Bianca Klettke, "How Does the Mind Construct and Represent Stories?" in Melanie C. Green, Jeffrey J. Strange, and Timothy C. Brock, eds., *Narrative Impact*, Mahwah, NJ: Erlbaum, 2002.

Gritton, Eugene, Paul K. Davis, Randall Steeb, and John Matsumura, *Ground Forces for a Rapidly Employable Joint Task Force*, Santa Monica, Calif.: RAND Corporation, 2000.

Haag, Chet, Ivans Chou, and Burce Preiss, "Variable Resolution Modeling," in Alex F. Sisti and Dawn A. Trevisani, eds., *Proceedings of SPIE*, Vol. 4716: *Enabling Technologies for Simulation Science VI*, 2002, pp. 218–228.

Haimes, Yacov, *Risk Modeling, Assessment, and Management*, New York: John Wiley & Sons, 1998.

Hammond, John S., Ralph L. Keeney, and Howard Raiffa, *Smart Choices: A Practical Guide to Making Better Decisions*, New York: Broadway Books, 2002.

Hastie, Reid, and Nancy Pennington, "Explanation-Based Decision Making," in Terry Connolly, Hal R. Arkes, and Kenneth R. Hammond, eds., *Judgment and Decision Making: An Interdisciplinary Reader*, 2d ed., Cambridge, UK: Cambridge University Press, 2000, pp. 212–228.

Heacox, Nancy J., Michael L. Quinn, Richard T. Kelly, and John W. Gwynne, *Decision Support System for Coalition Operations: Final Report*, San Diego, Calif.: SPAWAR Systems Center, 2002.

Henry, Ryan, "Defense Planning: Building Top-Level Capabilities," unpublished briefing, Washington, DC: Office of the Secretary of Defense, 2004.

Heuer, Richard J., *Psychology of Intelligence Analysis*, Washington, DC: Central Intelligence Agency, 1999.

Heuer, Richard J., "Strategic Deception and Counterdeception: A Cognitive Process Approach," *International Studies Quarterly*, Vol. 25, No. 2, 1981, pp. 294–327.

Hillestad, Richard, and Paul K. Davis, *Resource Allocation for the New Defense Strategy: The DynaRank Decision Support System*, Santa Monica, Calif.: RAND Corporation, 1998.

Hillestad, Richard, John Owens, and Donald Blumenthal, "Experiments in Variable Resolution Combat Modeling," in Jerome Bracken, Moshe Kress, and Richard Rosenthal, eds., *Warfare Modeling*, Alexandria, VA: Military Operations Research Society, 1995, pp. 63–86.

Hinsley, Francis H., E. E. Thomas, C. F. Ransom, and R. C. Knight, *British Intelligence in the Second World War*, New York: Cambridge University Press, 1979.

Hirt, Edward R., Frank R. Kardes, and Keith D. Markman, "Activating a Mental Simulation Mind-Set Through Generation of Alternatives: Implications for Debiasing in Related and Unrelated Domains," *Journal of Experimental Psychology*, Vol. 40, No. 3, 2004, pp. 373–383.

Hitch, Charles, "Analysis for Air Force Decisions," in Edward S. Quade (ed.), *Analysis for Military Decisions*, New York: North-Holland, 1966, pp. 13–23.

Hitch, Charles J., and Roland N. McKean, *Economics of Defense in the Nuclear Age*, New York: Holiday House (published originally by RAND Corporation and Harvard University Press in 1960), 1965.

Hodgkinson, Gerard P., Nicola J. Brown, A. John Maule, Keith W. Glaister, and Alan D. Pearman, "Breaking the Frame: An Analysis of Strategic Cognition and Decision Making Under Uncertainty," *Strategic Management Journal*, Vol. 20, No. 10, 1999, pp. 977–985.

Hoeber, Francis P., *Military Applications of Modeling: Selected Case Studies*, New York: Gordon and Breach, for Military Operations Research Society, 1981.

Hogarth, Robin M., "Beyond Discrete Biases: Functional and Dysfunctional Aspects of Judgmental Heuristics," *Psychological Bulletin*, Vol. 90, No. 2, 1981, pp. 197–217.

Holland, John H., *Emergence: From Chaos to Order*, Cambridge, MA: Perseus Books, 1998.

Holland, John H., and Heather Mimnaugh, *Hidden Order: How Adaptation Builds Complexity*, New York: Perseus Publishing, 1996.

Horrigan, Timothy, *Configural Theory and the Mathematical Modeling of Combat*, Chicago, IL: Horrigan Analytics, HAS 91-17-1, 1991.

Hughes, Wayne, "Combat Science: An Organizing Study," *Military Operations Research*, Vol. 1, No. 1, 1994, pp. 45–57.

Hughes, Wayne (ed.), *Military Modeling*, 2d ed., Alexandria, VA: Military Operations Research Society, 1989.

Hura, Myron, Gary McLeod, Richard Mesic, Philip Sauer, Jody Jacobs, Daniel Norton, and Thomas Hamilton, *Enhancing Dynamic Command and Control of Air Operations Against Time Critical Targets*, Santa Monica, Calif.: RAND Corporation, 2002.

Ilachinski, Andrew, "ISAAC Web Page," Center for Naval Analyses, online at http://www.cna.org/isaac/, as of 2004.

Irandoust, Hengameh, "Attitudes for Achieving User Acceptance: Explaining, Arguing, Critiquing," 7th International Command and Control Research and Technology Symposium, Quebec City, Quebec, Canada, 2002.

Jacobi, Dennis, Don Anderson, Vance von Borries, Adel Elmaghraby, Mehmed Kantardzic, and Rammohan Ragade, "Building Intelligence in Third-Generation Training and Battle Simulations," in Alex F. Sisti and Dawn A. Trevisani, eds., *Proceedings of SPIE*, Vol. 5091: *Enabling Technologies for Simulation Science VII*, 2003, pp. 154–163.

Janis, Irving L., *Groupthink: Psychological Studies of Policy Decisions and Fiascoes*, 2d ed., Dallas, TX: Houghton Mifflin Co., 1982.

Jervis, Robert, *Perception and Misperception in International Politics*, Princeton, NJ: Princeton University Press, 1976.

Jervis, Robert, Richard Ned Lebow, and Janice Gross Stein, *Psychology and Deterrence*, Baltimore, MD: The Johns Hopkins University Press, 1985.

Johnson, Dominic D.P., Richard W. Wrangham, and Stephen Peter Rosen, "Is Military Incompetence Adaptive? An Empirical Test with Risk-Taking Behaviour in Modern Warfare," Evolution and Human Behavior, Vol. 23, No. 4, 2002, pp. 245–264.

Johnson, Stuart E., William A. Owens, and Martin C. Libicki, *Dominant Battlespace Knowledge*, Honolulu, HI: University Press of the Pacific, 2002.

Joint Staff, *Joint Vision 2010*, Washington, DC: Department of Defense, 1996.

Kahan, James P., and Amnon Rapoport, *Theories of Coalition Formation*, Hillsdale, NJ: Lawrence Erlbaum Associates, 1984.

Kahan, James P., D. Robert Worley, and Cathleen Stasz, *Understanding Commanders' Information Needs*, Santa Monica, Calif.: RAND Corporation, 2000.

Kahneman, Daniel, "Maps of Bounded Rationality: A Perspective on Intuitive Judgment and Choice (Nobel Prize Lecture)," online at http://www.nobel.se/economics/laureates/2002/kahneman-lecture.html, as of 2002.

Kahneman, Daniel, and Amos Tversky, "On the Reality of Cognitive Illusions: A Reply to Gigerenzer's Critique," *Psychological Review*, Vol. 103, No. 3, 1996, pp. 528–531.

Kahneman, Daniel, and Amos Tversky, "Prospect Theory: An Analysis of Decision Under Risk," *Econometrica*, Vol. 47, No. 2, 1979, pp. 263–291.

Kaplan, Steven E., J. Hal Reneau, and Stacey Whitecotton, "The Effects of Predictive Ability Information, Locus of Control, and Decision Making Involvement on Decision Aid Reliance," *Journal of Behavioral Decision Making*, Vol. 14, No. 1, 2001, pp. 35–50.

Kauffman, Stuart A., *The Origins of Order: Self-Organization and Selection in Evolution*, New York: Oxford University Press, 1993.

Keeney, Ralph, and Howard Raiffa, *Decisions with Multiple Objectives*, New York: Wiley, 1976.

Kent, Glenn A., and David A. Ochmanek, *A Framework for Modernization Within the United States Air Force*, Santa Monica, Calif.: RAND Corporation, 2003.

Kent, Glenn A., and William E. Simons, *A Framework for Enhancing Operational Capabilities*, Santa Monica, Calif.: RAND Corporation, 1991.

Khong, Yuen Foong, *Analogies at War: Korea, Munich, Dien Bien Phu, and the Vietnam Decisions of 1965*, Princeton, NJ: Princeton University Press, 1992.

Klayman, Joshua, and Kaye Brown, "Debias the Environment Instead of the Judge: An Alternative Approach to Reducing Error in Diagnostic (and Other) Judgment," *Cognition*, Vol. 49, No. 1, 1993, pp. 97–122.

Klein, Gary, *Sources of Power: How People Make Decisions*, Cambridge, MA: MIT Press, 1998.

Koehler, Jonathan, "The Base Rate Fallacy Reconsidered: Descriptive, Normative, and Methodological Challenges," *Behavioral and Brain Sciences*, Vol. 19, No. 1, 1996, pp. 1–53.

Krause, Lee S., Dean Christopher, and Lee A. Lehman, "Multiagent Intelligent Systems," in Alex F. Sisti and Dawn A. Trevisani, eds., *Proceedings of SPIE*, Vol. 5091: *Enabling Technologies for Simulation Science VII*, 2003, pp. 58–65.

Kuehberger, Anton, "The Influence of Framing on Risky Decisions: A Meta-Analysis," *Organizational Behavior and Human Decision Processes*, Vol. 75, No. 1, 1998, pp. 23–55.

Kulick, Jonathan, and Paul K. Davis, "Judgmental Biases in Decision Support for Air Operations," in Alex F. Sisti and Dawn A. Trevisani, eds., *Proceedings of SPIE*, Vol. 5091: *Enabling Technologies for Simulation Science VII*, 2003a, pp. 260–271.

Kulick, Jonathan, and Paul K. Davis, *Modeling Adversaries and Related Cognitive Biases*, Santa Monica, Calif.: RAND Corporation, RP-1084, 2003b.

Lee, John D., and Katrina A. See, "Trust in Automation: Designing for Appropriate Reliance," *Human Factors*, Vol. 46, No. 1, 2004, pp. 50–80.

Lempert, Robert J., "A New Decision Science for Complex Systems," *Proceedings of the National Academy of Sciences Colloquium*, Vol. 99, Suppl. 3, 2002.

Lempert, Robert J., Steven W. Popper, and Steven C. Bankes, *Shaping the Next One Hundred Years: New Methods for Quantitative Long-Term Policy Analysis*, Santa Monica, Calif.: RAND Corporation, 2003.

Levy, Jack S., "Applications of Prospect Theory to Political Science," *Synthese*, Vol. 135, No. 2, 2003, pp. 215–241.

Lewin, Roger, *Complexity: Life at the Edge of Chaos*, Chicago, IL: University of Chicago Press, 2000.

Light, Paul C., *The Four Pillars of High Performance*, New York: McGraw-Hill, 2004.

Lindblom, Charles Edward, "The Science of Muddling Through," in Stella Z. Theodolou and Matthew A. Cahn, eds., *Public Policy: The Essential Readings*, Englewood Cliffs, NJ: Prentice Hall, 1995, pp. 113–127.

Lipshitz, Raanan, "Knowing and Practicing: Teaching Behavioral Sciences at the Israel Defense Forces Command and General Staff College," *Journal of Management Studies*, Vol. 20, 1983, pp. 121–140.

Lipshitz, Raanan, Gary Klein, Judith Orasanu, and Eduardo Salas, "Taking Stock of Naturalistic Decision Making," *Journal of Behavioral Decision Making*, Vol. 14, No. 5, 2001, pp. 331–352.

Llinas, James, Ann Bisantz, Colin Drury, Younho Seong, and Jiun-Jim Jian, *Studies and Analyses of Aided Adversarial Decision-Making, Phase 2: Research on Human Trust in Automation*, Buffalo, NY: State University of New York at Buffalo, 1998.

Loftus, Elizabeth, and Katherine Ketcham, *The Myth of Repressed Memory: False Memories and Allegations of Sexual Abuse*, New York: St. Martin's Press, 1994.

Lopes, Lola L., and Greg C. Oden, "The Rationality of Intelligence," in Ellery Eells and Tomasz Maruszewski, eds., *Probability and Rationality: Studies on L. Jonathan Cohen's Philosophy of Science*, Amsterdam, The Netherlands: Rodopi, 1991, pp. 199–223.

Lucas, Thomas, "The Stochastic Versus Deterministic Argument for Combat Simulations: Tales of When the Average Won't Do," *Military Operations Research Journal*, Vol. 5, No. 3, 2000, pp. 9–28.

Luce, R. Duncan, and Howard Raiffa, *Games and Decisions: Introduction and Critical Survey* [1957], New York: Dover Publications, 1989.

Macedonia, Michael R., "Games Soldiers Play," *IEEE Spectrum Online*, March 7, 2005.

MacGregor, Douglas A., "Future Battle: The Merging Levels of War," *Parameters*, Vol. 22, No. 4, 1992, pp. 33–47.

Mandeles, Mark, Thomas C. Hone, and Sanford S. Terry, "Managing Command and Control," *The Persian Gulf War*, Westport, CT: Praeger, 1996.

March, James G., with the assistance of Chip Heath, *A Primer on Decision Making: How Decisions Happen*, New York: The Free Press, 1994.

Matsumura, John, Randall Steeb, John Gordon, Tom Herbert, Russell W. Glenn, and Paul Steinberg, *Lightning over Water: Sharpening America's Capabilities for Rapid-Reaction Missions*, Santa Monica, Calif.: RAND Corporation, 2001.

May, Ernest R., *"Lessons" of the Past: The Use and Misuse of History in American Foreign Policy*, New York: Cambridge University Press, 1973.

McCrabb, Maris (Buster), "Explaining 'Effects,'" unpublished paper for the United States Air Force Research Laboratory, 2001.

McEver, Jimmie, Paul K. Davis, and James H. Bigelow, *EXHALT: Interdiction Model for Exploring Halt Capabilities in a Large Scenario Space*, Santa Monica, Calif.: RAND Corporation, MR-1137-OSD, 2000.

McKelvey, Bill, "Complexity Theory in Organization Science: Seizing the Promise or Becoming a Fad," *Emergence: A Journal of Complexity Issues in Organizations and Management*, Vol. 1, 1999.

McQuay, William K., "Distributed Collaborative Environments for Virtual-Capability Planning," in Alex F. Sisti and Dawn A. Trevisani, eds., *Proceedings of SPIE*, Vol. 5091: *Enabling Technologies for Simulation Science VII*, 2003, pp. 66–77.

Meadows, Donella H., Jørgen Randers, and Dennis L. Meadows, *The Limits to Growth: The 30-Year Update*, White River Junction, VT: Chelsea Green Publishing Company, 2004.

Mellers, Barbara A., Alan Schwartz, and Alan D.J. Cooke, "Judgment and Decision Making," *Annual Review of Psychology*, Vol. 49, 1998, pp. 447–477.

Meystel, Alex, and James Albus, *Intelligent Systems: Architecture, Design and Control*, New York: Wiley, 2002.

Millot, Marc Dean, Roger C. Molander, and Peter Wilson, *The "Day After . . ." Study: Nuclear Proliferation in the Post-Cold War World*, Vol. II: *Main Report*, Santa Monica, Calif.: RAND Corporation, MR-253-AF, 1993.

Mintz, Alex, "Foreign Policy Decision Making in Familiar and Unfamiliar Settings: An Experimental Study of High-Ranking Military Officers," *Journal of Conflict Resolution*, Vol. 48, No. 1, 2004, pp. 49–62.

Mintzberg, Henry, *Rise and Fall of Strategic Planning*, New York: Free Press, 1994.

Mintzberg, Henry, Bruce Ahlstrand, and Joseph Lampel, *Strategy Safari: A Guided Tour Through the Wilds of Strategic Management*, New York: Free Press, 1998.

Miser, Hugh J., and Edward S. Quade, eds., *Handbook of Systems Analysis*, New York: North-Holland, 1988.

Moffat, James, *Complexity Theory and Network Centric Warfare*, Washington, DC: Department of Defense, CCRP Publication Series, 2003.

Molander, Roger, Peter Wilson, David Mussington, and Richard Mesic, *Strategic Information Warfare Rising*, Santa Monica, Calif.: RAND Corporation, MR-964-OSD, 1998.

Moore, Louis, Daniel Gonzales, David Matonick, Chris Pernin, and Robert Uy, *Improving the C⁴ISR Analysis Capabilities of the Systems Effectiveness Analysis Simulation (SEAS)*, Santa Monica, Calif.: RAND Corporation, AB-557-AF, 2001.

Moore, Nancy Y., Laura H. Baldwin, Frank Camm, and Cynthia R. Cook, *Implementing Best Purchasing and Supply Management Practices: Lessons from Innovative Commercial Firms*, Santa Monica, Calif.: RAND Corporation, 2002.

Morgan, M. Granger, and Max Henrion, *Uncertainty: A Guide to Dealing with Uncertainty in Quantitative Risk and Policy Analysis*, New York: Cambridge University Press, 1990.

Morrison, Jeffrey G., Richard T. Kelly, Ronald A. Moore, and Susan G. Hutchins, "Implications of Decision Making Research for Decision Support and Displays," in Janis Cannon-Bowers and Eduard Salas, eds., *Making Decisions Under Stress: Implications for Individual and Team Training*, Washington, DC: APA Books, 2000, pp. 375–406.

Muir, Bonnie M., and Neville Moray, "Trust in Automation: Part II. Experimental Studies of Trust and Human Intervention in a Process Control Simulation," *Ergonomics*, Vol. 39, No. 3, 1984, pp. 429–460.

Murdock, Clark A., *The Role of Red Teaming in Defense Planning*, McLean, VA: Hicks and Associates, Working Paper #03-3, DART Working Paper, 2003.

Murray, Williamson, *Red Teaming: Its Contribution to Past Military Effectiveness*, McLean, VA: Hicks and Associates, Defense Adaptive Red Team (DART) Report, 2002.

Mynatt, Clifford R., Michael E. Doherty, and Ryan D. Tweney, "Consequences of Confirmation and Disconfirmation in a Simulated Research Environment," *Quarterly Journal of Experimental Psychology*, Vol. 30, 1978, pp. 395–406.

National Academy of Sciences, *Making the Nation Safer: The Role of Science and Technology in Countering Terrorism*, Washington, DC: National Academy Press, 2002.

National Research Council, *The Role of Experimentation in Building Future Naval Forces*, Washington, DC: National Academy Press, 2004.

National Research Council, *Modeling and Simulation in Manufacturing and Defense Acquisition: Pathways to Success*, Washington, DC: National Academy Press, 2002.

National Research Council, *Network Centric Naval Forces*, Washington, DC: Naval Studies Board, National Academy Press, 2000.

National Research Council, *Technology for the United States Navy and Marine Corps: 2000–2035*, Vol. 9: *Modeling and Simulation*, Washington, DC: National Academy Press, 1997.

Neyland, David L., *Virtual Combat: A Guide to Distributed Interactive Simulation*, Mechanicsburg, PA: Stackpole Books, 1997.

Nicolis, Grégoire, and Ilya Prigogine, Self-Organization in Nonequilibrium Systems: From Dissipative Structures to Order Through Fluctuations, New York: John Wiley & Sons, 1977.

Nisbett, Richard E., David H. Krantz, Christopher Jepson, and Geoffrey T. Fong, "Improving Inductive Inference," in Daniel Kahneman, Paul Slovic, and Amos Tversky, eds., *Judgment Under Uncertainty: Heuristics and Biases*, New York: Cambridge University Press, 1982, pp. 445–459.

Nitze, Paul H., "Reflections on the Cuban Missile Crisis," online at http://www.cosmos-club.org/journals/1998/nitze.html, as of 1998.

Ochmanek, David A., Edward Harshberger, David E. Thaler, and Glenn A. Kent, *To Find, and Not to Yield: How Advances in Information and Firepower Can Transform Theater Warfare*, Santa Monica, Calif.: RAND Corporation, 1998.

Owens, William A., and Edward Offley, *Lifting the Fog of War*, New York: Farrar Straus Giroux, 2000.

Paté-Cornell, M. Elizabeth, and Seth D. Guikema, "Probabilistic Modeling of Terrorist Threats: A Systems Analysis Approach to Setting Priorities Among Countermeasures," Ithaca, NY: Cornell University, Working paper of the Department of Management Science and Engineering, 2002.

Patel, Vimla L., David R. Kaufman, and Jose F. Arocha, "Emerging Paradigms of Cognition in Medical Decision-Making," *Journal of Biomedical Informatics*, Vol. 35, No. 1, 2002, pp. 52–75.

Payne, John W., James R. Bettman, and Eric J. Johnson, The *Adaptive Decision Maker*, New York: Cambridge University Press, 1993.

Payne, Wilbur B., "Ground Combat Models," in Wayne Hughes (ed.), *Military Modeling*, 2d ed., Alexandria, VA: Military Operations Research Society, 1989, pp. 129–144.

Pedersen, Dorothy, James R. Van Zandt, Alan L. Vogel, and Marlene R. Williamson, "Decision Support System Engineering for Time Critical Targeting," *Proceedings of the Command & Control Research & Technology Symposium*, Newport, RI: Naval War College, 1999.

Price, Paul C., and Eric R. Stone, "Intuitive Evaluation of Likelihood Judgment Producers: Evidence for a Confidence Heuristic," *Journal of Behavioral Decision Making*, Vol. 17, No. 1, 2004, pp. 39–57.

Quade, Edward S. (ed.), *Analysis for Military Decisions*, New York: Rand-McNally/North-Holland, 1966.

Quade, Edward S., and Wayne I. Boucher, eds., *Systems Analysis and Policy Planning: Applications in Defense*, New York: Elsevier North-Holland, 1968.

Quade, Edward S., and Grace M. Carter, eds., *Analysis for Public Decisions*, 3d ed., New York: North-Holland, 1989.

Quinn, James B., *Strategies for Change—Logical Incrementalism*, Homewood, IL: Irwin, 1980.

Raiffa, Howard, *Decision Analysis: Introductory Lectures on Choices Under Uncertainty*, Reading, MA: Addison-Wesley, 1968.

Roberts, Donald F., Ulla G. Foehr, and Victoria Rideout, *Generation M: Media in the Lives of 8–18 Year Olds*, Washington, DC: Kaiser Family Foundation, 2005.

Rosen, Julie A., and Wayne L. Smith, "Influence Net Modeling with Causal Strengths: An Evolutionary Approach," Presented paper, Monterey, Calif.: U.S. Naval Postgraduate School, 1996.

Rumsfeld, Donald, *Report of the Quadrennial Defense Review*, Washington, DC: Department of Defense, 2001.

Saaty, Thomas L., *Multicriteria Decision Making: The Analytic Hierarchy Process*, Pittsburgh, PA: RWS Publications, 1990.

Samuels, Richard, Stephen Stich, and Michael Bishop, "Ending the Rationality Wars: How to Make Disputes About Human Rationality Disappear," in Renee Elio (ed.), *Common Sense, Reasoning and Rationality*, New York: Oxford University Press, 2002, pp. 236–268.

Sanchez, Susan M., and Thomas W. Lucas, "Exploring the World of Agent-Based Simulations: Simple Models, Complex Analysis," *Proceedings of the Winter Simulation Conference*, Orlando, FL, 2000.

Sanna, Lawrence J., Norbert Schwarz, and Shevaun L. Stocker, "When Debiasing Backfires: Accessible Content and Accessibility Experiences in Debiasing Hindsight," *Journal of Experimental Psychology: Learning, Memory, and Cognition*, Vol. 28, No. 3, 2002, pp. 497–502.

Santos, Eugene, Jr., "A Cognitive Architecture for Adversary Intent Inferencing: Structure of Knowledge and Computation," in Alex F. Sisti and Dawn A. Trevisani, eds., *Proceedings of SPIE*, Vol. 5091: *Enabling Technologies for Simulation Science VII*, 2003, pp. 182–193.

Sawyer, Kathy, "Witness Chides NASA in Assessing Risk; Ex-Space Official Cites Review of Problem-Plagued 1999 Columbia Mission," *The Washington Post*, March 7, 2003, p. A08.

Schmitz, Walter, Otto Reidelhuber, and Klaus Niemeyer, "Some Long-Term Trends in Force Structuring," in Reiner K. Huber (ed.), *Modeling and Analysis of Conventional Defense in Europe: Assessment of Improvement Options*, New York: Plenum Press, 1984, pp. 141–165.

Schultz, James V., *A Framework for Military Decision Making Under Risks*, Masters thesis, Montgomery, AL: Maxwell AFB, School of Advanced Airpower Studies, 1997.

Serfaty, Daniel, Elliot E. Entin, and R. R. Tenney, "Planning with Uncertain and Conflicting Information," in Stuart E. Johnson and Alex H. Levis, eds., *Science of Command and Control: Part II, Coping with Complexity*, Fairfax, VA: AFCEA Press, 1989, pp. 91–100.

Serfaty, Daniel, Jean MacMillan, Elliot E. Entin, and Eileen Entin, "The Decision-Making Expertise of Battle Commanders," in Caroline E. Zsambok and Gary Klein, eds., *Naturalistic Decision Making*, Mahwah, NJ: Lawrence Erlbaum Associates, 1997, pp. 233–246.

Shafir, Eldar, and Robin A. LeBoeuf, "Rationality," *Annual Review of Psychology*, Vol. 53, 2002, pp. 491–517.

Shanteau, James, "Cognitive Heuristics and Biases in Behavioral Auditing: Review, Comments, and Observations," *Accounting, Organizations, and Society*, Vol. 14, No. 1/2, 1989, pp. 165–177.

Silverman, Barry G., "Unifying Expert Systems and the Decision Sciences," *Operations Research*, Vol. 42, No. 3, 1994, pp. 393–413.

Simon, Herbert, *Models of Bounded Rationality*, Vol. 1, Cambridge, MA: MIT Press, 1982a.

Simon, Herbert, *Models of Bounded Rationality*, Vol. 2, Cambridge, MA: MIT Press, 1982b.

Simon, Herbert, "Rational Decision-Making in Business Organizations," *Nobel Lectures, Economics 1969–1980*, Singapore: World Scientific Publishing, 1978.

Simon, Herbert A., "Rational Choice and the Structure of the Environment," *Psychological Review*, Vol. 63, No. 2, 1956, pp. 129–138.

Sinnreich, Richard Hart, *Red Team Insights from Army Wargaming*, McLean, VA: Hicks and Associates, Defense Adaptive Red Team (DART) Working Paper 02-3, 2002.

Sisti, Alex F., "Dynamic Situation Assessment and Prediction (DSAP)," in Alex F. Sisti and Dawn A. Trevisani, eds., *Proceedings of SPIE*, Vol. 5091: *Enabling Technologies for Simulation Science VII*, 2003, pp. 10–16.

Skov, Richard B., and Steven J. Sherman "Information-Gathering Processes: Diagnosticity, Hypothesis-Confirmatory Strategies, and Perceived Hypothesis Confirmation," *Journal of Experimental Social Psychology*, Vol. 22, No. 2, 1986, pp. 93–121.

Smith, Edward R., *Effects Based Operations: Applying Network Centric Warfare in Peace, Crisis, and War*, Washington, DC: Department of Defense, Command and Control Research Program, 2003.

Sokolowski, John A., *Modeling the Decision Process of a Joint Task Force Commander*, Suffolk, VA: Old Dominion University, 2003.

Speier, Cheri, and Michael G. Morris, "The Influence of Query Interface Design on Decision-Making Performance," *MIS Quarterly*, Vol. 27, No. 3, 2003, pp. 397–423.

St. John, M., J. Callan, and S. Proctor, *Tactical Decision-Making Under Uncertainty: Experiments I and II*, San Diego, Calif.: Space and Naval Warfare Systems Center, Technical Report 1821, 2000.

Stanley, William, "Assessing the Affordability of Fighter Aircraft Force Modernization," in Paul K. Davis (ed.), *New Challenges for Defense Planning: Rethinking How Much Is Enough*, Santa Monica, Calif.: RAND Corporation, 1994, pp. 565–592.

Stanovich, Keith E., and Richard A. West, "Individual Differences in Reasoning: Implications for the Rationality Debate?" *Behavioral and Brain Sciences*, Vol. 23, No. 5, 2002, pp. 645–726.

Starr, Stuart, "Assessing Military Information Systems," in Stuart E. Johnson, Martin Libicki, and Gregory Treverton, eds., *New Challenges, New Tools for Defense Decisionmaking*, Santa Monica, Calif.: RAND Corporation, 2003, pp. 299–322.

Sterman, John D., *Business Dynamics: Systems Thinking and Modeling for a Complex World*, Boston, MA: McGraw-Hill/Irwin, 2000.

Stone, Eric R., Winston R. Sieck, Benita E. Bull, J. Frank Yates, Stephanie C. Parks, and Carolyn J. Rush, "Foreground: Background Salience: Explaining the Effects of Graphical Displays on Risk Avoidance," *Organizational Behavior and Human Decision Processes*, Vol. 90, No. 1, 2003, pp. 19–36.

Swett, Charles, "Transforming How We Plan: Capabilities-Based Planning and the New Approach to Defense Planning Scenarios" (dated November 18, 2002), Presentation at the 71st Military Operations Research Society, Washington, DC: Department of Defense, Office of the Deputy Assistant Secretary (Resources and Plans), 2003.

Szyperski, Clemens, *Component Software: Beyond Object-Oriented Programming*, 2d ed., New York: Addison-Wesley, 2002.

Tarter, C. John, and Wayne K. Hoy, "Toward a Contingency Theory of Decision Making," *Journal of Educational Administration*, Vol. 36, No. 3, 1998, pp. 221–228.

Tatarka, Christopher J., "Overcoming Biases in Military Problem Analy-sis and Decision-Making," *Military Intelligence Professional Bulletin*, January–March 2002.

Treshansky, Allyn, and Robert McGraw, "MRMaide: A Mixed Resolution Modeling Aide," in Alex F. Sisti and Dawn A. Trevisani, eds., *Proceedings of SPIE*, Vol. 4716: *Enabling Technologies for Simulation Science VI*, 2002, pp. 190–200.

Trevisani, Dawn, Alex F. Sisti, and Michael J. Mayhew, "Model Abstraction and the Simulation Sandbox," in Alex F. Sisti and Dawn A. Trevisani, eds., *Proceedings of SPIE*, Vol. 4716: *Enabling Technologies for Simulation Science VI*, 2002, pp. 211–217.

Trevisani, Dawn, Alex F. Sisti, and Jerome H. Reaper, "Joint Synthetic Battlespace for Decision Support," in Alex F. Sisti and Dawn A. Trevisani, eds., *Proceedings of SPIE*, Vol. 5091: *Enabling Technologies for Simulation Science VII*, 2003, pp. 132–140.

Tversky, Amos, and Daniel Kahneman, "Extensional Versus Intuitive Reasoning: The Conjunction Fallacy in Probability Judgment," *Psychological Review*, Vol. 90, No. 4, 1983, pp. 293–315.

Tversky, Amos, and Daniel Kahneman, "The Framing of Decisions and the Psychology of Choice," *Science*, Vol. 211, 1981, pp. 453–458.

Tversky, Amos, and Daniel Kahneman, "Judgment Under Uncertainty: Heuristics and Biases," *Science*, Vol. 185, 1974, pp. 1124–1131.

Ubel, Peter, "Identifying and Reducing Cognitive Biases Created by Decision Aids," University of Michigan, online at http://www.med.umich.edu/pihcd/projects/decisionaid/decisionaid.htm, as of 2002.

Uhrmacher, Adelinde, Paul A. Fishwick, and Bernard Zeigler, "Special Issue: Agents in Modeling and Simulation: Exploiting the Metaphor," *Proceedings of the IEEE*, Vol. 89, No. 2, full volume, 2001.

Uhrmacher, Adelinde M., and William Swartout, "Agent-Oriented Simulation," in M. Obaidat and G. Papadimitriou, eds., *Applied System Simulation: Methodologies and Applications*, Kluwer Academic Publishers, 2003.

U.S. Air Force, Deputy Chief of Staff, Plans and Operations, *JFACC Primer*, 2d ed., Washington, DC: United States Air Force, 1994.

van de Riet, Odette, *Policy Analysis in Multi-Actor Policy Settings: Navigating Between Negotiated Nonsense and Superfluous Knowledge*, Delft, Netherlands: Eburon Publishers, 2003.

van Dijk, Eric, and Marcel Zeelenberg, "The Discounting of Ambiguous Information in Economic Decision Making," *Journal of Behavioral Decision Making*, Vol. 16, No. 5, 2003, pp. 341–352.

Verheij, Bart, "Anchored Narratives and Dialectical Argumentation," Paper presented at the International Conference on Artificial Intelligence and Law, St. Louis, MO, 2001.

Vick, Alan, David Orletsky, Bruce Pirnie, and Seth Jones, *The Stryker Brigade Combat Team: Rethinking Strategic Responsiveness and Assessing Deployment Options*, Santa Monica, Calif.: RAND Corporation, MR-1606-AF, 2002.

von Neumann, John, and Oskar Morgenstern, *Theory of Games and Economic Behavior*, 3d ed. [c. 1944], Princeton, NJ: Princeton University Press, 1953.

Wagenhals, Lee, Insub Shin, and Alexander E. Levis, *Executable Models of Influence Nets Using Design/CPN*, Fairfax, VA: Systems Architectures Laboratory, George Mason University, 2001.

Wainfan, Lynne, and Paul K. Davis, *Challenges in Virtual Collaboration: Videoconferencing, Audioconferencing, and Computer-Mediated Communications*, Santa Monica, Calif.: RAND Corporation, 2004.

Waldrop, Mitchell M., *Complexity: The Emerging Science at the Edge of Order and Chaos*, New York: Simon & Schuster, 1992.

Warden, John A., III, *The Air Campaign: Planning for Combat*, Washington, DC: Pergamon Brassey's, 1989.

Weinberg, Steven, *Dreams of a Final Theory: The Scientist's Search for the Ultimate Laws of Nature*, New York: Vintage Books, 1994.

Wickens, Christopher D., and Justin Hollands, *Engineering Psychology and Human Performance*, New York: Prentice-Hall, 1999.

Wilkening, Dean, "A Simple Model for Calculating Ballistic Missile Defense Effectiveness," *Science & Global Security*, Vol. 8, No. 2, 1999, pp. 183–215.

Wit, Emst-Jan C., *Risk and Responsibility*, Amsterdam, The Netherlands: University of Amsterdam, Dissertation, 1997.

Wojtkowski, Wita, and W. Gregory Wojtkowski, "Storytelling: Its Role in Information Visualization," Presented paper, *Proceedings of the Fifth European Systems Science Congress*, Crete, Greece, 2002.

Woolsey, Robert E. D., and Richard L. Hewitt, eds., *Real World Operations Research: The Woolsey Papers*, Marietta, GA: Lionheart Publishing, 2003.

Wrangham, Richard W., "Is Military Incompetence Adaptive?" *Evolution and Human Behavior*, Vol. 20, No. 1, 1999, pp. 3–18.

Yang, Jian-Bo, and Madan G. Singh, "An Evidential Reasoning Approach for Multiple Attribute Decision Making with Uncertainty," *IEEE Transactions on Systems, Man, and Cybernetics*, Vol. 24, No. 1, 1994, pp. 1–18.

Yaniv, Ilan, "Receiving Other People's Advice: Influence and Benefit," *Organizational Behavior and Human Decision Processes*, Vol. 93, No. 1, 2004, pp. 1–13.

Zachary, Wayne, "Decision Support Systems: Designing to Extend the Cognitive Limits," in Martin G. Helander (ed.), *Handbook of Human-Computer Interaction*, Amsterdam: Elsevier Science Publishers, 1998.

Zeigler, Bernard, *Multifaceted Modeling and Discrete Event Simulation*, Ontario, Calif.: Academic Press, 1984.